MW01107419

MINING FOR GOLD
·IN YOUR RELATIONSHIPS

RESOLVE
couple conflict from beneath the surface

RESTORE
loving connection

INSPIRE
enduring intimate pleasure

Melva Thomas Johnson, L.S.M.W.
and
Jesse Johnson, M.A.

Published by
Couples Publishing

Published by

COUPLES PUBLISHING
512 South Washington, Suite 329
Royal Oak, MI 48067

For information about special discounts for bulk purchases, please contact

Special Sales, Couples Publishing
512 South Washington #329, Royal Oak, MI 48067

or email at
CouplesPublishing@PersonalTransformations.Com

or by phone at
1-877-552-1161

ISBN: 0 9793741 0 3

Book Cover
designed by Dominic Pangborn

Manufactured in the United States of America

A NOTE TO OUR READERS

The names of those persons used in this book are fictitious. We have made a conscious attempt to modify any identifying characteristics to protect the privacy and confidentiality of those who agreed to share their stories. The cases described are often composites – drawn from various situations over time. The dialogue represents either the gist of what was said or a representation of it. The important thing was to share what appeared to be those universal human experiences that are common among a great many people in long term, committed relationships. As you read these stories, our hope is that you gain insight into your own relationship challenges and benefit by using the Mining For Gold process to transform your own relationship.

The Mining for Gold (MFG) Process as well as the information contained in this book is intended for educational purposes only. It should not be used as a substitute for psychological and/or medical consultation with a competent health care professional. The book's contents may be used as an adjunct to a rational and responsible healthcare program prescribed by a healthcare practitioner. It is not intended as psychotherapy, a diagnosis, prescription, or treatment of any health disorder.

Readers are to understand that this book is designed to assist them in understanding their relationships and providing guidelines for improving them. Reader also accepts sole responsibility for the decisions made the results and the consequences regarding their use of this material. The authors and publishers are in no way liable for any misuse of the material.

DEDICATION

We lovingly dedicate this book to....

our sons, Paul and Brian, who have given us tremendous joy throughout our life journey together as a family. We are proud of the men that you have become

our parents—the late Wyman and Celestine Thomas, Geneva and the late Jesse Johnson, Sr. Their love, care, nurturing, teaching, values, and support provided a solid foundation for growth and development upon which we could build our lives

our siblings—Paulette Roberts, Fred Johnson, Gayle Patterson, Wyman Thomas and Louis Thomas and their families for their genuine unconditional love and support

we feel honored and privileged for being a part of such a phenomenal extended family of aunts, uncles, nieces, nephews, and cousins

the six couples that generously shared their stories for this book

our ancestors on whose shoulders we now stand. We deeply appreciative and affectionately dedicate this book in their memory

all of our ministers and spiritual teachers who have helped us along our spiritual journey

a host of colleagues and friends—far too numerous to mention individually. We deeply appreciate your caring, support, and our special relationship

and we dedicate this book to our readers in hope that the Mining for Gold process will enable you to create extraordinary relationships.

ACKNOWLEDGMENTS

We would like to express our very deep and sincere gratitude to the following persons....

To our many wonderful clients, students, workshop and lecture participants who have enriched our lives in such incredible ways over our 30 years in private practice

To Harville Hendrix, Ph.D. and Helen LaKelly Hunt, Ph.D. the founders of the Imago Relationship theory and therapy—the foundation for this book, and authors of the best selling books, <u>Getting the Love You Want</u>, <u>Keeping the Love You Find, Giving the Love That Heals</u>, <u>Receiving Love</u>, <u>Faith and Feminism</u>, and numerous other works already written and those in process for your friendship, encouragement, suggestions, advice, inspiration and ongoing support

To Marianne Williamson, author of several bestselling books, including, <u>Everyday Grace</u>, <u>A Return To Love</u>, <u>Illuminata</u>, <u>A Woman's Worth</u>, *and* <u>Healing The Soul Of America</u>; for her ongoing encouragement and support of our work and this book from the very beginning stages of writing

To Maya Kollman, M.A., Imago Relationship, Master Trainer and Maureen Brine, Reg.N., I.C.A.D.C., Imago Clinical Instructor, for providing incredible certification trainings for us

To Martha Baldwin Beveridge, MSSW, BCD, author of <u>Loving Your Partner Without Losing Yourself</u>, for her encouragement and support, and for referring us to Priscilla Stuckey, our first editor and coach for writing this manuscript

To Priscilla Stuckey, Ph.D., for holding our hands through the first several drafts and sharing her expertise and wisdom to keep us on track

To Joyce Buckner, Ph.D., author of <u>Making Real Love Happen: The New Era of Intimacy</u>, for always being encouraging and supportive of us and for her numerous contributions to our understanding of couples relationship theory, therapy, and practice

To Pat Love, Ed.D., author of <u>How to Improve Your Marriage Without Talking About It: Finding Love Beyond Words</u>, for commitment to the exploration of the physiological, psychological, and behavioral influences that affect the relationship between couples and her consistent, genuine, and deeply appreciated encouragement and support

To Tom Kerr for helping our words to come alive in a way that supported us to relay our message to our readers in the way that we intended

To Dominic Pangborn, of Pangborn Design, an extremely creative and gifted artist and designer, for his design of our book cover, his support, and friendship

To our wonderful friends and supporters who were so willing to write their personal endorsements for this book

To our friends Arnold Patent, author of <u>You Can Have It All</u>, and Selma Patent, co-author with Arnold of <u>The Treasure Hunt</u>, for our life journey together in both living by and sharing Universal Principles with each other and others

To the Rev. Shaheerah Shephens, our longtime friend who is our ongoing supporter and cheerleader for whatever we do and for being there for us all the time, any time.

To John and Anna Gagern, for their friendship, enthusiastic support, and for zapping us with "Reiki" to keep our energy up while we worked on this project

To the Conway family—Andrew, Barbara, Matt, and Alex for truly being family for us

To Sid and Kay Berkowitz. We are grateful to our dear friend Sid—our first professional psychotherapy trainer, who has provided us with guidance, wisdom, and unrelenting support. And we are deeply appreciative to Kay for being such a genuine and authentic friend and colleague, who has consistently demonstrated her friendship in numerous loving expressions of caring and support

To Rosalind Griffin, M.D. and Sam Williams. We are so deeply humbled and appreciative of your friendship and ongoing support. You always seem to find a way to enhance whatever project we're undertaking. We cherish our times shared, the fun, laughter, and the numerous ways you enrich our lives

To Burton Bacher, M.D. and Mrs. Helen Bacher. We have searched in vain to find the words adequate enough to express our heartfelt gratitude for your life long and ongoing love, friendship, generosity, encouragement and support on so many levels—both personally and professionally. Thank you

To Gail Parker, Ph.D. and Tom Johnson, M.D., M.B.A., for the wonderful opportunity for us to come together again I a very special way, for our friendship, our plans for the future, and the excitement of continuing to share our lives and life journey

Darren Johnson, M.S.O.D., for being so generous with his time, ideas, experience, and support in guiding us through the terrain of completing the details involved in publishing this book.

To Darold Gholston, B.A, author of <u>The Art of Romance</u> for his friendship, encouragement, and support by staying on us for the past six and a half years to make sure we completed this project and for giving valuable tips, resources, and incredible support in numerous ways

To Rasheda Williams, B.A., our friend who has consistently been there for us, for staying on us for the past six and a half years to make sure we completed the project, for giving valuable writing tips, assisting with editing and also providing incredible support in so many ways

To David Goldstein, M.D., author of several books, including, <u>The Guide to Healthy Eating</u>, for not only giving us moral support and encouragement, but also teaching us how to format the manuscript for printing

To our fellow colleagues, parents, community persons and students in those public and private schools where we have worked—for the wonderful experiences shared and the accomplishments made on behalf of our children.

TABLE OF CONTENTS

Chapters:

FOREWORD

Marriage has been around for a long time, but only recently has it been seen as a resource for healing and wholeness making. We are honored by the authors of MINING FOR GOLD to write a foreword for a book that so clearly describes such a marriage. Sharing stories of couples from their practice and their own storage, we are privileged to witness the process and outcome of couples transforming their relationship.

While we do not know if hunter-gatherer "bonded-pairs" who existed millions of years ago were formally married or what difficulty they may have had in their relationships, cultural anthropologists tell us that these early couples bonded for survival by "sharing" the resources each could bring to the family—carbohydrates in the form of berries and nuts from the women who gathered and protein from the hunters who brought the meat. Their bond also provided a balanced meal for the children and protected them from predators. Their relationship problems, if they had any, were probably resolved by finding another mate, as is the case with contemporary couples!

Somewhere about thirty to fifteen thousand years ago, these wanderers discovered how to grow plants and herd animals, and they settled down into encampments that eventually became villages, towns, cities, nation states and empires—but the economy was organized around agriculture until the Industrial Revolution. With fields to tend and animals to herd, having many children to help with the work was important. With the ability to store food, the idea of property and the need to protect it arose. The concept was eventually extended to women and children. Children, being perceived as the property of the parents, were paired with the children of other families who would enhance social status and increase economic resources, thus giving rise to the arranged marriage. The purpose of this marriage was economic and social status and stability. Conflicted couples in these marriages, unlike their forbearers who probably replaced a difficult partner with a new one, could not so easily replace their partners because of all the imposed sanctions. Instead of divorce, they met their emotional needs by having affairs with secret lovers, like a large number of contemporary couples.

This arrangement slowly came to an end in the 18th century with the arrival of democracy which by law guaranteed the freedom of expression and personal choice. For centuries, everyone belonged to someone else who determined their destiny; in a few short decades everyone belonged to themselves and their destiny was determined by their free choices. This included the right to chose whom one would marry. Survival and social concerns were no longer criteria for selecting a partner. The choice no longer in the hands of the parents, adult children followed their hearts and selected someone to whom they were attracted, with whom they fell in love. Thus the third form of marriage to appear in the history of the world emerged: marriage by choice. Marriage became a private affair; its purpose to serve personal and psychological needs.

Although unknown by the participants who fell in love, their choice of a partner was fueled by unmet needs from childhood. What seemed like a conscious choice was really determined by unconscious forces beyond their control. The degree of romantic attachment was an indication the severity of early wounding by parents, and the movement towards marriage was fueled with the unconscious expectation that the chosen partner would meet those needs. No having an instructional manual, couples did not know that their conflicts reflected unresolved needs from their childhood. Conflict became the norm and marriage became unstable.

Whereas marriages in the past were stable because of social and religious sanctions—it became a sacrament of the Roman Catholic Church in the sixth century although reduced in status to a sacred relationship by the Protestant Reformation in the 16th century—by the middle of the 20th century couples began to abandon their marriages, producing a divorce rate hovering around 50% for the past sixty years.

Until the early part of the 20th century, couples who were in trouble received advice, counsel and admonitions from religious professionals. No other resources were available until the advent of marriage counseling by non-religious professionals early in the last century. For the first time in history, couples were offered help not by advice or exhortation but by attempting to help them understand their relationship and work out solutions that fit them uniquely. In the early stages, some marital therapists sought to help couples resolve conflict in their marriage by learning communication skills and teaching them methods of conflict resolution, problem solving, negotiation and compromise. Other marital therapists, bred to believe that all relational problems were manifestations of problems within the persons in conflict, sought to help people resolve their intra-psychic conflicts with the assumption that when they resolved their personal problems they would have good marriages. The success of these therapies was dismal, about 35%.

A shift in direction came in the latter quarter of last century which assigned marital problems to dysfunction in the family system; the system and the transactions between partners and other members of the family—if there were any—became the patient. This was a tectonic shift in therapeutic consciousness. Marital therapy shifted from the location of problems in the inner world of the client to the interpersonal. What happens between persons became more important than what happens inside the persons. The new paradigm of relational therapy came into being and enlarged the resources for healing. While conflict resolution and intra-psychic therapy endures, the shift toward relational therapy is rapidly gaining grown as the therapy of choice for couples.

The couples therapy demonstrated by Melva and Jesse Johnson in their book, MINING FOR GOLD, is an instance of this new paradigm that focuses on the relationship rather than the individuals involved. It is a relational process known as Imago Relationship Therapy. Imago agrees with the intra-psychic model that persons in conflict with their partners have a troubled inner world and with the conflict resolution model that teaches communication skills as a resource for problem solving. And it is congruent with the systems model that focuses on altering interpersonal dynamics and transactions to repair the individual.

But for Imago therapy, the couple's relationship itself is the healing resource. The "between" heals the "within." To activate this process, Imago Therapy helps couples transform their relationship by engaging them in a process which transforms their consciousness. This process is Imago Dialogue, singular therapeutic intervention of Imago Relationship Therapy. The outcome of using the dialogue process does not merely help couples improve their relationship or get "better." It includes and them beyond communication skills and conflict resolution. It also includes and goes beyond healing and wholeness. By helping partner's accept and celebrate the "otherness" of each other, thus freeing each other from the prison of idealization and consequent disappointment and from the distortions of their projections, it helps them transform their relationship into a conscious partnership. Using Imago Dialogue, couples rupture their fusion with each other and become separate persons who can then deeply connect with each other at deep levels.

The achievement of connection with each other heals the rupture in their relationship caused by the intrusion of unresolved issues from childhood and in the process heals the rupture within caused by childhood trauma. Imago Dialogue helps couples create a safe space called the "sacred between" in which their defenses can relax so they can meet each other with compassion and empathy. The outcome is that unmet childhood needs are identified and met; undeveloped potential in each partner evolves and an original wholeness is restored. Restored connection dissolves conflict, replaces it with creative tension and the result is relaxed joyfulness and the experience of full aliveness: our true nature. This is the "gold" the authors find hidden in the depths of conflict, the treasure that is brought to light in the Imago Dialogue process.

The stories of the couples in this excellent book illustrate the power of the Imago process to transform couples in profound ways. The depth of their sharing is very touching. We honor their courage to remove the husks that obscured the gold in their relationship, for taking the journey and sharing it with others.

We hope this book will attract a large audience of couples and clinical professionals. Couples who read these stories will learn a new way of loving. Therapists who read the book will learn a powerful process to use in their own lives and to help couples replace the tide of divorce and populate society with healthy couples and happy children. We honor the authors for their success and for offering the fruits of their work to the world.

Harville Hendrix, Ph.D.

PREFACE

Despite couples' best efforts, they often find themselves trapped in old patterns of conflict and unable to change them. Without intervention, these negative reactive patterns predict their relationship's eventual demise.

We help couples resolve their differences and resume sharing the love they desire— through a simple, effective process for decoding common conflicts. By integrating the theories of Harville Hendrix, PhD, author of the best selling, Getting the Love You Want, and founder with his wife, Helen LaKelly Hunt, Ph.D. of imago relationship therapy and those of other noted relationship experts, we help couples dig beneath their anger and frustrations to discover each one's deeper emotional needs. The Mining for Gold process is a proven, simple formula for decoding the patterns of relationship conflicts. Using it, any couple can stop hurtful, reactive behaviors, understand each other more deeply, and create a stronger, more loving connection.

This book documents the experiences of 14 real-life clients of ours who used the Mining for Gold (MFG) process to work through long-standing resentments and dig beneath the surface of habitual conflicts. By showing the MFG process at work, we shed light on the negative reactive patterns that are so destructive to relationships.

As these seven couples demonstrate, it is easy to become aware of our critical behavior reactions and create new, effective solutions. MFG is a powerful process for change. If utilized consistently, any couple can implement MFG immediately and reap its benefits.

The issues these couples addressed represent universal dynamics. Through them, readers can gain insight into their own frustrated needs and take steps to become liberated from emotional distress. Armed with a greater awareness of the interplay in their own relationships, readers can learn new ways of asking for what they want while they restore loving connections with greater security, intimacy, and passion.

INTRODUCTION

Falling in Love

How wonderful it felt! Finally, after a long search and countless disappointments, you suddenly thought you'd met your soul mate. And being so happy, you wanted to return that love. If you ever found yourself annoyed with your beloved you apologized right away and moved back into your loving – and fun-loving – connection. You made a commitment to each other, believing that your love would conquer everything.

But somewhere between two minutes to two years later, the quality of that romantic connection began to change. Your heart, once throbbing with desire, pounded from frustration. Little upsets that you once handled quickly took longer to resolve – or never got resolved. Your partner displayed more of those traits that push your buttons. *How could my beloved say that? How could the one I love ever act like that?* You felt your affection shrink from irritation.

What happened?

At this point – understandably – you reacted by letting your significant other know what was on your mind. You had your first real argument. And then another, until they became part of a pattern. Accused of being critical and judgmental, you countered with, "How dare you!"

Frustrated, you urged your partner to open up and talk, but met a cold shoulder. Feeling an impasse, you disconnected, not knowing what else to do. You had no place to go with your feelings, and may have felt more lonely that when you were actually alone.

What went wrong?

After a cooling-off period, the two of you began to talk again, but not about the original issue. You knew you had a problem, but you chose not to mention it – at least for the time being. After all, you had developed an endless list of frustrations. No need to wake a sleeping bear or open Pandora's box. It felt easier to handle other things and let them divert your attention from the issue at hand, at least for the moment.

But you used to get along so well. How did you change into feeling so terribly frustrated by each other? Why did your partner stop listening to you and start talking *for* you? Did you choose the wrong person?

Welcome to Stage Two of your relationship! The romantic phase has faded and the power struggle ensues. The problem is that most couples don't realize that this is a *natural* transition within any committed, long-term relationship. Far too often, couples hit this stage like a wall of bricks and react by breaking up and calling it quits.

More than 50 percent of first marriages end in divorce. Of couples who stick it out, more than 75 percent report that unresolved conflicts create ongoing dissatisfaction in important areas of their relationship. They describe habitual interactions with their partners as "hot," "cold," or "lukewarm"; and those patterns often repeat themselves in any new relationship they might seek after divorce.

Fighting distracts couples from the underlying causes of their conflicts. Most remain at the level of unidentified symptoms, unaware that the root of the problem lies deep beneath the surface. Criticizing, blaming each other, declaring themselves right and their partner wrong – ultimately these common reactions can destroy what could have otherwise become an immensely rewarding shared journey through life.

Focusing on surface conflicts and discontents – all symptoms of a bigger problem and work still to be done – keeps the couple from progressing to the next natural stage of their relationship. Over time, the Mining for Gold process helps to build a foundation of emotional support that lets each partner feel loved and cared about. We've seen again and again that the MFG process help couples achieve the loving relationship they both desire.

We know the scenarios so well, because we've heard them hundreds of times from our clients. And since we're married to each other, much of what we hear mirrors our own experience.

What Goes So Terribly Wrong In Our Relationships?

In an ideal world, your first painful experience would teach you to make better decisions in the future. But mysteriously, most of us repeat the same hurtful scenarios over and over—with the same predictable outcomes.

Why do we subject ourselves to repeated disappointments? It is because too many of us are love-starved and long for an intimate connection with someone who understands and supports us. And we don't give up the search for a lifelong partner to fill that void and give us the love we want.

The worst kind of loneliness is to feel alone when you're with someone. You may try to distract yourself by diverting time and attention to other things. You may feel even more intensely disappointed because you once enjoyed that loving connection you always desired, and then it vanished – again. Many of us end relationships through separation or divorce – others remain together, bearing the discomfort as best they can.

Yes, you can enjoy joyful moments if you choose to stay together, but you deserve more than brief periods of connection. You *can* learn to sustain a better connection that endures. But to create mutually safe, effective communication that lets each partner be heard requires knowledge and skills you were most likely never taught – until now.

This book offers what you need to create a loving relationship, and then continually sustain it over time.

Couples who cling to the Hollywood myth of "living happily ever after" are shocked to find that no matter how much they love each other, frustrations – obstacles to intimacy – are inevitable. Since you can't avoid them, the Mining for Gold process is a useful way to deal with them effectively, while also using them to gain positive and valuable benefits.

What is Your Story?

Many of us have some idea of the traits our "soul mate" should have. And consciously and unconsciously, we search for that ideal person.

What were you looking for in a love partner? How did you meet your current partner or your most recent ex who had those traits? At that time, what was going on in your life: at work, with your family, with your friends?

When you first began to be attracted, what about this person got your attention? How did the two of you communicate that attraction? When did you begin to date? When did your relationship become serious? If you married, when did the topic of marriage come up? What was the proposal like? How about the courtship and wedding plans? What was the honeymoon like? How long did the romantic stage last?

When did the quality of your relationship begin to change? What was it like being together? How was your partner different? How were you different? What is or was your greatest frustration with that person? How do you or did you address those frustrations? Where did you seem to get stuck?

Many of us fantasize about the relationship of our dreams, but never exercise the same imagination regarding what to do when our relationships are in trouble. We tend to think more about growing old together and less about the work it takes to get there.

Initially, we got caught up in the fantasy like many couples. Before we got together, each of us made a list of the positive traits we wanted in our "soul mate." Shortly after making the lists, we began to notice those traits in each other so we decided to get together and become a couple. It didn't take long before we were going through the predictable relationship stages—from attraction to romance on the way toward becoming a blended family. Not long after getting married and living under the same roof, we began to notice little things that we had not paid much attention to before. Each of us had our own annoying idiosyncrasies—particular habits and ways of doing things that resulted in varying degrees of irritation. That is when the really hard work began. We had to find ways to successfully manage our differences.

All couples must find ways to deal with their differences. If your partner squeezes toothpaste from the middle of the tube, and you from the bottom, one simple solution is for each of you to have your own toothpaste, to eliminate irritation. But repetitive, emotionally charged conflicts require a great deal more in terms of behavioral investigation and modification. To handle those more serious conflicts, MFG is a powerfully effective tool.

A Life-Changing Moment

We were moving along, enjoying our life together, and continuing to build our counseling practice. Both of us were seasoned therapists with over 22 years of experience. Over our professional lives, we had helped people work through their issues at home, at work, and in the community. But our least favorite clients were couples.

We studied various approaches to marriage therapy, trying different strategies from a number of theorists. Our success was minimal at best. Eventually, we decided it wasn't ethical to invite couples to come to our office and pay us to take sides as they fought the same way they did at home. It seemed that we only served to reinforce whatever frustrations and rage they were already experiencing. During some sessions couples became extremely agitated and we had to struggle to calm them down and guide them in a more positive direction.

But one factor was always consistent – these couples in distress were experiencing tremendous emotional pain. We could empathize because of our own failed marriages, and we decided that we needed to take a different approach. We began working with each partner individually, and after several individual sessions, brought them together – only to watch them start fighting all over again!

Finally we decided that couples therapy just wasn't for us. And then we saw Harville Hendricks on Oprah.

Oprah's crew had taped Dr. Hendrix in action conducting one of his Imago Couples Weekend workshops. Oprah also interviewed couples who talked quite candidly about the kinds of problems that had plagued their relationships. Some admitted that without help, they would certainly have divorced.

Harville explained the dynamics that had kept them mired in frustration, and the couples told of amazing insights and positive change.

Afterwards, we called the show to get more information about Harville's work and inquire about possible training. As a prerequisite for training, we had to attend an Imago weekend workshop for couples. The same workshop Melva saw on Oprah.

The workshop was a wonderful, growth-inspiring weekend. We learned healing tools and life-changing processes that offered marvelous benefit for us and for our clients.

After 23 years of marriage, we thought we knew each other thoroughly. And we did, but still needed to dig beneath our ongoing conflicts. We were really clueless about what our basic frustrations and conflicts were, and what they were trying to teach us. Unfolding before us – and vague at first – was a blueprint to help us grow into higher-functioning individuals. And it showed us the way to relate as never before.

We left the workshop feeling more deeply connected. But when those same old frustrations surfaced in our day-to-day interactions, we couldn't sustain our good feelings. We each expected the other to change, convinced that one of us was "right" and the other was "wrong."

Finally we had to stop blaming and criticizing each other. Whenever our buttons got pushed, we had to move through our reactivity and overcome our natural impulse to see each other as the enemy. When we finally used the tools we had learned from Harville there was an immediate shift toward a welcome emotional reconnection.

What Changed for Us?

Before, we would have a fight, not fully understanding why. And we had no reliable way of resolving our differences. But what we learned during the Imago Couples Workshop weekend and the subsequent Imago Clinical Training for Therapists gave us practical tools to help us understand our conflicts and work through them in mutually satisfying ways. After an argument, we used to stay angry and emotionally disconnected for days. Even when we tried to re-connect, the issue was simply pushed aside, not resolved. It would always come up again with greater intensity, because we'd carry all our previous anger into future situations. Imago allowed us a chance – and a system – to resolve issues faster and re-establish loving connections more quickly.

Imago Relationship Therapy gave us the concepts and tools we needed. We now spend a great deal more time being affectionate, supportive, and appreciative of each other.

As therapists, Imago has given us the foundation to help couples achieve significant, desirable differences in their relationships. Couples have become our favorite clients. Imago's powerful tools help them manage their reactivity, express their needs and fears, and have their partners understand their emotional feelings.

It's truly wonderful to watch couple after couple move through their conflicts and connect heart to heart.

The closer you feel to another person, the safer and vulnerable you'll be. So committed relationships are where frustrations grow the most troublesome. And if frustrations continue unresolved, eventually they will impact your relationship's stability and erode its foundation.

If you're reading this book, it's likely you expect a lot from yourself and from those closest to you. Those expectations are sometimes unrealistic, but every time your partner doesn't meet them, you're apt to express your annoyance in no uncertain terms. If your frustrations intensify, you may start looking for ways to exit the relationship – emotionally, physically, or legally.

The simple but extremely effective MFG process has helped thousands of couples to resolve their differences and "different-ness." We offer a step-by-step process to turn repetitive, ongoing annoyances into deeper, loving connections that transform frustration into a wealth of opportunity.

Isn't that why you two got together in the first place?

The couples who contributed their experience to this book

Each of the couples who contributed their case histories to this book attended a 22-hour weekend workshop that we conducted. Digging beneath their surface frustrations, they realized what they really needed from each other. And they finally learned to ask for it in a way that vastly increased the likelihood that they would get it, and continue to get it, for the duration of their relationship.

Over the following year, they participated in a monthly 90-minute follow-up session that we also drew upon for this book.

ALLOW ME TO INTRODUCE TO YOU
Jesse and Melva Johnson

Dear Reader:

You are about to read the words and hear the voices of Jesse and Melva Johnson. It occurred to me that the knowing of their spirits and voices would connect you more closely with their written ideas.

Allow me to introduce them to you in a way that may strengthen your understanding and enhance the pleasure you are about to experience.

They began the journey of their careers as wonderful listeners, caring persons, and warm human beings. Their study and experiences and passion for the kind of communication that adds to closeness and loving feelings led them to their current work and to the writing of this book.

Hear the voice of Melva...sweet, melodic, energetic, and responsive. Always encouraging, at times she pauses to select just the right word or phrase.

When Jesse enters the dialog, his pace is slower; his deep mellow voice is as soothing and supportive as are his expressive eyes.

And, when you read their own personal stories, don't be surprised if you hear a quiet husky chuckle from Jesse or an open-hearted laugh from Melva, eyes dancing, head tossed back, often smoothing the side of her hair.

Kay Berkowitz, LMSW, ACSW

CHAPTER 1
BLAME AND CRITICISM: FROM ROMANCE TO RAGE

"It Wasn't Supposed to Be Like This"

Sobbing, Ada curled up on the bed, her head buried in the pillow. Ben sat stiffly in the den, remote control in hand, silently surfing channels. Three small children tiptoed back and forth in the kitchen, trying not to disturb their parents.

That very afternoon, Ada had gotten a promotion at work and a huge raise. She came home to share her good news and found Ben winding down in front of the TV, after a stressful day. She plopped down on his lap, hugging and kissing him. "You can't imagine what happened today!" she said enthusiastically.

He froze beneath her, not looking to meet her gaze, his attention fixed on the television.

Ada was shocked at his lack of response. "He's not interested", she told herself. Infuriated, she lashed out. "How can you just sit there and say nothing?"

Isn't he interested in what is important to me?

Feeling overwhelmed by her accusations, Ben began to shout "What are you talking about? You're always getting on my case. Does everything have to be about you?"

Ada got up and glared at him. "So, your priorities don't include me?"

Exasperated, she stormed out of the den to their bedroom.

I thought he loved me. Does he even care about me? How can my husband be so cruel?

Ben was upset, but stared at the TV as the thoughts and emotions churned inside his brain. *She is so unreasonable. I had a miserable day at work. Doesn't she even care? How could she just storm in here like that and demand that I listen to her? She used to be interested in me. She was understanding. When I came home, she would ask about my day and encourage me to relax. Now she only wants to talk about herself. When did she become so self-centered?*

Over the course of a 15-year marriage, Ada and Ben had argued plenty. Like most couples, they didn't realize that the tension they were playing out was a predictable and inevitable dynamic that nearly every couple eventually experiences. They hadn't expected the romantic phase of their relationship to fade. And it faded faster than they could have imagined; suddenly replaced by routine frustrations that constantly bubbled to the surface. What they failed to comprehend was that they were not alone – almost every close and enduring relationship goes through such phases. It is the norm, not the exception.

The Power Struggle: From Romance to Conflict

When they first started dating, the attraction was powerful, emotionally rewarding, and full of passionate chemistry and pleasurable companionship. And because of how intensely Ada and Ben initially bonded with one another, a power struggle over need fulfillment was sure to follow.

They truly loved and cared for each other, but as their relationship budded and blossomed, they were enamored by it and casually overlooked the behaviors and differences that would later create a tug of war.

Eventually, as those differences became apparent, they began struggling to work out mutually satisfying solutions. Each communicated their personal opinions and judgments of the situation, negotiating for power. Both of them felt justified and determined to convince the other of their point of view. They argued, trying to get the other partner to yield. But in order for one partner to be right, the other had to be wrong. The solutions they envisioned were mutually exclusive, and they reached a lose-lose stalemate, as their mutual mediation methods hit a stone wall.

Each believed that the other was at fault and unwilling to compromise. When painted into a corner, one would resort to threats and issue disturbing ultimatums:

> Maybe we need a little time apart.
> Maybe we should think about seeing other people for a change.
> Maybe we should just get a divorce.

People who stay together generally respond in one of two ways:

Either one partner becomes assertive the way Ada did, seeking resolution by insisting "we need to talk ", or they go into a protective shell like Ben, feeling that the other person is being confrontational and too intense. They sidestep the problem by passively retreating. The result is that both are frustrated and feel they aren't getting any cooperation. They freeze each other out, ignoring each other's reactions, and nobody talks. Neither is willing to call it quits, despite the fact that what used to be shared warmth becomes a mutual cold shoulder or downright drama.

Ada and Ben had been aware of their seething discontent for a long time. Ada was concerned about the increasing frequency of her involuntary knee jerk reactions, and she began to panic because she felt like she was losing control of her emotions. Ben knew he was shutting down, and the less he talked about it to Ada, the more his mind became agitated and his mood melancholy.

Ada and Ben were perfect candidates for the MFG process.

The Mining for Gold Process

The MFG process is simple:

You stop in the midst of frustration, take a deep breath, calm down, and pay attention to whatever you're experiencing and feeling in the moment of *right now*. You explore whatever insights or awareness surface. You try to pinpoint the specific interaction that led to the conflict, clarifying what exactly it was about your partner's behavior that frustrated you. You examine the way he or she pushed your buttons, and how you reacted, but you don't react. Once you become aware of what's on the surface of the conflict you are better equipped to dig past the tip of the iceberg and examine the underlying emotions.

Okay, so it's simple *on one level*. We didn't say it was a walk in the park. But with practice it can be.

To show how it's done, we will outline the steps of the same MFG process we used with six couples we worked with over a period of 12 months. And we'll add our own story, a true account of how we used – and continue to use – this process successfully in our own relationship.

Each couple had very specific—yet quite common—unresolved issues that put a considerable strain on their respective relationships. Ada and Ben are simply a prototype of the seven couples who applied the MFG method.

As I told Ada when she first called, "The essence of our work is to decode the specific blueprint for personal healing and growth that underlies common conflicts. Once that blueprint is decoded, we coach you—as a couple—to follow that blueprint, dissolve the conflict, and embrace the possibilities your relationship offers."

Fooled by Appearances

When we try to maintain close relationships in Stage Two, the Power Struggle phase, we have a tendency to focus only on the difficulties. When our partner consistently expresses frustration or shuts down, we interpret the behavior as an attack, a judgment, or a criticism.

When couples can't resolve their issues, they blame each other and react in ways that add fuel to the volatile atmosphere of discontent, intensifying each partner's discomfort. They throw emotional gasoline on the fire of conflict, and the relationship ultimately goes up in smoke.

Power struggles in any long-term relationship may be unavoidable, but are only a visible manifestation of specific problems that can be solved. Conflict is inevitable, and provides a *golden* opportunity for deeper interpersonal understanding and connection. But most couples are unaware that their conflicts are merely symptoms, and they never move forward to the third, natural stage of treating the source of discontent and going to the more intimate level of what we call "mature love."

The two identifying characteristics of mature love are *Safety* and *Connection*. Each partner is offered a conscious, conflict-free way of relating, and an agreement to *end all criticism*. Each commits to becoming a source of safe refuge and emotional support for the other. The commitment is reinforced day by day, situation after situation, moment to moment, and the result is that each partner feels cared about and loved.

As many couples have discovered, MFG offers a positive and proactive alternative that is far better than staying embroiled in squabbles as the surface tension mounts. Both partners begin to uncover the reasons behind their reactivity. Rather than reacting or lashing out, they learn to respond and listen without feeling threatened or defensive. By mining for "gold"— the love buried deep within—each discovers what they both yearn for, and together learn to give and receive the love that each desires.

Read on, and you'll learn exactly how to do it.

CHAPTER 2
BEGINNING WITHIN: FROM REACTIVE TO REFLECTIVE

"Looking More at Me, Less at You"

A few couples who seek counseling may have fallen "out of love," but the overwhelming majority still care deeply for each other.

The major problems for most are:

1) dealing with a daily failure to resolve emotional conflicts.
2) coping with the pain that those conflicts create.

They finally decide to seek professional help, often out of a sense of desperation. Their hope is that they will learn better ways to communicate, solve problems, and enjoy more fulfilling lives.

Most couples frustrate each other from time to time— but still share many memorable moments of peaceful and loving connection. They generally push their frustrations aside after conflict—until a similar situation occurs and the problems percolate back to the surface.

As a result of pushing things under the rug, they then find themselves dealing with an accumulation of frustrations. Anger simmers, ready to surface when triggered. A healthy focus upon daily routines is undermined by a subtext of preoccupation with unresolved issues. Interest accumulates on a debt you establish and then forget to service. Similarly, the frustrations that couples accumulate compound like financial interest, adding to the "principal" of the original problem, until the proverbial wolves are at the door and the couple's emotional resources are spent.

Such couples describe their relationships as being "up one minute, down the next." Despite their best efforts, they can't figure out how to resolve the back and forth conflict. Uncertain as to how their partners will relate at any given moment, they each feel insecure and see no end in sight.

While each partner waits for the other to apologize, both remain stuck.

Only when we move the focus away from our partner's behaviors and start looking at our own participation in the problem can we unlock the impasse and begin to reverse the cycle. It's not important who takes the first step, only that each person takes a hard look at his or her own role in contributing to the other's pain. And, invariably, digging within means finding unexpected fears and hurts— buried feelings that trigger reactive behavior. Emotional injuries can be surprisingly old and may go far back as far as childhood. Yet those age-old disappointments and unfulfilled longings often leak into present relationships to "justify" the current reactions that fuel our conflicts.

To identify our own buried longings, hurts, and fears throughout our own marriage— which has now lasted more than a quarter of a century—we've repeatedly used tools that we adapted from Imago Relationship Theory.

Ben and Ada Illustrate the Process

On the day of the appointment, Ben and Ada arrived together, 15 minutes early. We greeted the couple and invited them upstairs to our office. Ada walked briskly in front of Ben, checking over her shoulder as if she were making sure that he was keeping up with her.

Ben waited for Ada to sit down and then took his seat across the room from her. The session began with Melva asking what they wanted to accomplish during our meeting time.

"I want Ben to talk to me," said Ada. "He doesn't listen to me or support me anymore. I feel so frustrated." She glared at him, but he just sat stoically, arms crossed, not looking at her.

"Ben," Jesse asked, "why are *you* here? And what you would like to accomplish?"

"I'd like for Ada to get off of my case. She is always complaining and she talks too much. Her going on and on really gets to me."

It's important for any couple to focus on one frustration, on one area of conflict, at a time. Once we have a topic, we have the partners describe how each one's reactions of frustration impact upon the other. Ada was clearly annoyed, because she came to the session armed with a long list of complaints about Ben. He was relieved; having feared that his wife would only reenact in our office what they did at home, which would anger him until he withdrew, which got them nowhere.

After a brief discussion, Ben and Ada decided to explore the problem of blame and criticism. Ada volunteered to go first. Jesse made sure that Ben agreed to let her begin, and reassured him that he'd soon have a chance to have his say. But he explained that before Ben responded, it was his job to hear Ada tell how his behavior affected her. He was only to listen until she was finished.

Now that one complaint or frustration was identified, we could proceed to getting more specific details of the conflict.

Getting More Specific

Step 1: What Behavior in Your Partner Triggers an Intense Emotional Reaction in You?

"We want you to get beyond the ongoing issues that trouble you," Melva explained. "Ada, you might feel that Ben doesn't support you or listen to you. Ben, you might be frustrated with Ada's complaining, blaming and judging. Is that accurate?"

They both nodded in agreement. We then knew we were on target, and gave them a brief explanation of the MFG process.

"Anything would be better than what we go through," Ada said.

"If it will get Ada off my back, I'm all for it," Ben retorted.

Melva gave them an overview of the steps. Then we took turns coaching the couple through the process.

From the outset, we try to encourage a bit of objectivity. While one partner's behavior might be frustrating to the other, it might not seem as annoying to a third person. Most people can distinguish statements of personal preference ("I don't like the way you comb your hair") from objective standards that almost everyone agrees on ("I don't like it when you spit on the rug"). Therefore, there's often a gap between what *should* make an individual reactive, and what *does*.

"What is it that Ben actually says or does that frustrates you so?" Melva asked. "Describe, in one sentence, what feelings surface for you—*before* the blaming and criticism begins. Start off with, 'Ben, whenever you . . .' and then finish the sentence."

Answering this question is difficult for those who tend to think in generalities. For example, one partner might tell the other, "You don't love me." That's general, judgmental, and too vague. A more specific statement would be, ""You went fishing on the day of our anniversary, and made no plans for us to celebrate. I was deeply hurt." This describes a *particular* behavior that triggered an intense reaction.

Some believe that "If my partner really loved me, he [or she] would *know* what upsets me so." The truth is, our partners often don't know! They may see that we're upset, but not know why. Since few people want to inflict pain on those closest to them, it is important to identify exactly what your partner has done (or failed to do) that you find upsetting, and communicate it to them, before you proceed to the next step.

"Okay," Ada said. "Whenever you don't listen to me."

"You almost have it," we explained. "But Ben doesn't know what you mean. Give him an example. For instance, he didn't respond to your good news about your promotion. Start off with, 'When I came home the other night ...' "

"Ben, when I came home excited about my promotion, you just kept looking at television."

We confirmed: "That's it! His specific frustrating behavior was that you didn't get the response you were looking for about your promotion."

Jesse instructed Ben to repeat exactly what he had just heard Ada say. We call this "mirroring." It was vital for Ada to feel that he had heard her. Otherwise, she would have only become defensive, and communication would have broken down.

"You wanted to tell me about your promotion," Ben said. "But I ignored you and kept on watching television. Is that right?"

"Yes," Ada sighed in relief. She'd finally gotten through to him. "That's what happened!" Back when they were dating— during the romantic stage of their relationship—Ben's attentiveness had endeared him to Ada. Now, memories of their late night talks still bought tears to her eyes. But like all too many partners, Ada assumed that after they married, Ben would continue to listen whenever she had something important to share. She enjoyed feeling deeply connected to him for about two years—until their first child was born. Then, with greater demands on their time, things changed; and the more she needed Ben's attention and support, the more he withdrew. She'd begun to feel disappointed and hurt, feeling that Ben had broken an implicit promise.

But for reasons that he described later in the session, Ben had started making promises he couldn't keep. It was *his* behavior that triggered Ada's surface emotions, but whenever she confronted him, he shifted the guilt and blame onto her.

Describing clearly those behaviors that frustrate you, and also describing your own emotional response, is pivotal in beginning to identify your internal "feeling" experience. Helping couples to identify the "cause and effect" factor is the beginning of self-awareness. The cause is the frustrating behavior exhibited by one partner. The effect is the feeling response triggered within the other partner.

Identifying Ben's specific frustrating behavior would help Ada identify the surface emotion that prompted her reactive behavior—which was her part in their conflict. Describing *exactly* what Ben actually said or did would help her become aware of what, specifically, led to her knee-jerk reaction.

Step 2: Identify Your Surface-Level Emotional Feelings and Reactive Behavior

The next step in the MFG process involves describing in a single word such as "angry," "sad," or "frightened", the spontaneous emotion you feel when your partner frustrates you. But many find it hard to identify emotional *feelings*, as opposed to *thoughts* and *beliefs*. We often lump them all together, describing our emotions and feelings as "thoughts." Whenever you start to describe your "feelings" in a phrase or sentence, most likely you're "thinking," not *feeling*. So we didn't expect Ada to make these distinctions in her first session.

"When you are frustrated in this way," Jesse asked, "what emotions surface? What do you feel? Irritation? Disappointment?"

But Ada, still new to this step, elaborated on Ben's frustrating behavior as she was asked to do in step one. Melva tried to help her shift gears. "When Ben ignores you, what *one word* describes what you're feeling inside?"

Ada thought for a moment. "It's anger." We weren't surprised. Anger is the first feeling that many identify when learning to use this process.

"Ben, when you don't acknowledge me and then criticize me for getting upset, I feel angry. I work hard at the office, and getting some kind of acknowledgement means so much to me."

Ben started to defend himself, but Jesse stopped him. "It's important that you hear her entire story, without interruption. You'll have your chance, we promise."

Ben sat back, and Jesse asked him to repeat to Ada, as precisely as possible, what he'd heard her say. He did so, remarkably well. Our next question to Ada was "How do you react?" Frustrated couples generally react in a ways that only fuel their conflict, so Ada had to go deeper and describe what she *did* when she felt that this anger. But like many others who are asked this same question, she said, "I got angry."

But anger is an *emotion*, not a reactive *behavior*. "Be more specific," Melva coached. "When you felt angry, what did you say or do?"

"Oh, I yelled at Ben." That's what we were looking for—a word that described her role in keeping the conflict going. Ada couldn't realize the deep impact that raising her voice had on Ben, until it was his turn to tell how he experienced his side of their conflict.

Ada justified her yelling at Ben, as a natural response to his withdrawal. Justifying our behaviors may give us comfort, but it doesn't solve a broader problem or meet a deeper need. If Ada stayed on that level, it is likely that both of their frustrations would intensify. So to help them reach new insights and forge a stronger connection, we moved on to the next step of the MFG process.

Step 3: Finding the Hurt beneath Your Reactive Response

Getting angry usually grabs the attention of a significant other. And the anger that fuels reactive behavior usually masks some deeper hurt. When you lose emotional connection and intimacy, even for a moment, it can feel like a painful loss. Typically, that hurt and pain is the next feeling we uncover in the MFG process.

Ada didn't realize that she was hurting—pain wasn't part of her conscious vocabulary in describing her feelings to us. When she and Ben fought, she felt unsafe. This is typical of people who don't get in touch with their reactive behaviors. To become aware of her hurt and explore those deeper emotions, she needed a sense of safety and a coach to guide her through the process.

After offering her reassurance and emotional support, we asked "Besides anger, what do you feel when Ben withdraws, is critical, or breaks his promises?" We gave her time to respond. Ada took several minutes to become more consciously aware of an uncomfortable feeling she had suppressed for years—of her intense loneliness.

"I struggle to avoid that because it hurts so much." Ada began to cry and sob, and it was several minutes before she continued: "Even though Ben and the children aren't far away, every time he withdraws, I feel like I'm out there by myself. He just doesn't realize how much I need him in my life, and how lonely I feel when we're not emotionally together."

The moment was particularly poignant, because Ada was letting Ben hear how vulnerable she was. When people feel emotionally safe, they tend to reveal their deepest feelings, trusting that there will be no blaming or shaming for what they express.

Ben was maintaining eye contact with Ada, and softly repeated back to her what he had heard. He didn't wait for Melva to ask Ada if she wanted to say more, but asked, "What else do you want to tell me about how you're hurting?" Finally, for the first time in a long time, Ada felt she had his attention. "Remember when we were dating?" she asked, wiping her eyes. "I told you how awful it is for me to feel alone. When you said you'd always be here for me, I believed it. But I don't believe you now. When I need you most, I feel abandoned."

Now it was time to ask about the next layer of emotion—the fear (we use *Webster's* definition of fear: "any painful emotion excited by danger, the anticipation of impending catastrophe") that generally accompanies anyone's hurtful feelings.

"What do you imagine will occur if you continue to feel this way? What's the worst that could happen if you keep feeling lonely for the next year? Five years? 10 or 20 years?"

"I'd hate to think about it!" On some level, Ada knew the consequences.

"I know," said Melva. "But my hunch is, you've often thought about it. If Ben continues to criticize and break his promise of being there, what's the worst that could happen?"

Glancing at Ben, she quickly looked away, taking her time to feel safe enough to say aloud what she had resisted revealing to him until now. "The worst thing is that you'll interpret my being upset as criticism or blame, and you'll withdraw more. I'm afraid we won't be able to reconnect, because I'll drive you away, or I'll leave. Then I truly will be all alone, and I don't want that!"

What Ada had described thus far was only 10% of a bigger picture. Imago theory states that 90% of all recurring conflicts can be traced back to unfinished childhood business that people bring into their adult relationships.

We hypothesize that Ada felt the same hurt and fear before she met Ben. As we grow up, unhealed childhood experiences don't just fade away. They remain an unresolved, and out of our awareness. Some memories can be recalled in vivid detail; others are kept beneath our conscious awareness, because they are so painful. Regardless, these "unfinished" experiences surface in our current relationships, simmering beneath the surface of conflict. And they'll remain below the surface and unconscious until we learn how to recognize and address them. Even if we are aware, we may try to discount their influence in our present struggles and how we react to them: *That was way back then, and I'm not going to wake a sleeping beast.* However, the more dependent and vulnerable we felt toward those who caused us pain in the past, the greater the impact in our later life.

"Recall your earliest memory," Melva asked Ada, "when you felt a similar hurt at being abandoned—when you worried you might permanently lose connection with someone who was important to you at that time."

Ada's parents divorced when she was nine years old, and her father continuously broke his promises to her. She vividly recalled waiting for his weekend visits, only to have him call her mother at the last minute to say that he wasn't coming. She recalled how, at many times in her childhood and in previous adult relationships, she was ignored and not heard. Someone she loved withdrew. Once again she dissolved into tears.

Unlike Ada, some choose not to do this work because they prefer to avoid reliving the pain of these memories. But if your goal is a meaningful, mutually satisfying relationship, it is essential to the process. The taste of the medicine may be bitter, but the healthy results are worth the cure.

It was important for Ada to know her unmet childhood needs, because she was likely to want the same from Ben. "First of all," she recalled, "I didn't understand why my parents separated. That was a family secret. They were excellent providers, but I didn't understand why they didn't take the time to listen and understand me. That's the main thing I needed from them to feel loved and cared about. I needed my mother to support me and show that she was proud of me rather than criticize me." Her longing for feeling "cared about" was the "gold" she was seeking to uncover.

Just as Ada had wanted something specific from her parents, now she needed something very specific from Ben. Not receiving it triggered her unmet needs from the past, and she became reactive.

Once she could communicate it, it raised the possibility that Ben could hear and respond positively, letting her move past her reactive behaviors.

Making An Outrageous Request

Now that Ada consciously knew what she needed from Ben, Melva asked her to tell him—in the broadest terms possible. "Make the biggest, most absurd request you can think of."

Ada grinned. "Ben, I don't want you to withdraw from me ever again. I want you hanging on every word I say until I'm ready to stop talking, even if I want to talk all night."

They both begin to laugh at how impossible it was. Including terms like *always* and *forever* helps to verbalize in a broad way, and lets us become aware of what we really want, before we phrase our desires more specifically.

Ada was now ready to make a more realistic, specific request that would give Ben valuable information. Now she saw that when she grew angry with him, she was actually yearning for close connection. If he tried to meet her need for connection in a very specific way, it might help her start to heal old wounds.

"Ben, I want us to listen and understand each other when we talk." This was what she needed to restore their connection. In discovering those parts of her puzzle that make such profound differences, Ada had unearthed new awareness about what she'd always wanted. But she hadn't yet completed the MFG process, and still had more steps to take.

Step 4: Satisfy Your Needs by Making Specific Requests

Ada clarified that what she really wanted from Ben was time to talk about things that were important to her. After hearing her describe how her parents didn't listen, he understood. And he didn't want to cause Ada any further pain.

For him to meet her needs, she had to make three very specific requests about how she wanted Ben to behave, to replace the old ways that had infuriated her. Until Ada communicated the specific words and behaviors that she longed for, Ben might try to meet her wants and needs but still miss the mark, resulting in additional pain for her and frustration for him.

We call these three requests the "keys" that will unlock a person's heart and restore connection. Each request should be short —one or two sentences. It should be positive, without any negative words like *stop* and *quit*, and without absolutes like *always* or *never*. There should be a time limit on how long these requests should be fulfilled—for the next week or month, for example.

Formulating three requests sounds simple. But because it requires a new way of thinking about what you want, it can be a challenge. We're so used to saying what we *don't* want that we must train ourselves to think more positively. Secondly, many of us have been so disappointed that we stopped asking for what we wanted and now such requests make us feel uncomfortable. Learning what to ask for what you want and how to ask for it requires moving through the old patterns of criticism, blame and shame to teaching your partner how to restore connection with you by describing your needs in a positive and specific way. The better you enable your partner to meet your needs, the more fulfilling your relationship can become.

"Think about three ways," Melva said, "that Ben can listen to you so that you feel heard."

We asked for three requests because it provided Ben with more choices and less pressure. If he promised to do just one thing and he didn't follow through, it would only remind Ada of the times when her father didn't keep promises. So from Ada's three requests, Ben could choose the one that he felt most comfortable giving to her—not out of obligation, but out of his love for her.

To Ben, Jesse said, "As she makes each request, you must listen on two levels—to her words and your internal response—how you are feeling in your body. Then repeat each of her requests back to her."

After hearing Ada's three requests, Ben selected one that he could fulfill. It didn't really matter which he selected, because all three represented what Ada wanted. He couldn't go wrong, because if he followed through on any one of them, he'd satisfy Ada's core desire.

"For the next month," she said, "when I get home from work, I want 15 minutes to share with you any good news I might have. I want you to listen and explain to me what makes sense to you about my excitement."

Ben repeated to her what she said.

"Number two, for the next 30 days, I want you to prove that you're giving your full attention by maintaining eye contact while I'm sharing my good news. Also, I want you to ask me questions to show you're paying attention, and I want you to make a heartfelt statement that you're proud of me."

After Ben mirrored back Ada's second request, she continued.

"Number three, for the next 30 days, when you're not ready to hear my good news, I want you to set a time when you will be ready within 24 hours — and then follow through with the time we've set."

After Ben repeated Ada's third request, Melva coached him to rank each request as easy, difficult, or very hard to fulfill.

"Your first request," Ben told Ada, "giving you 15 minutes when you come home—would be hard. I need time to unwind. "Your second, to maintain eye contact is kind of hard. But asking questions is even harder, because I don't always know what to ask. But your third request is something I can do. After I regroup, I can let you know when I'm ready for you to share. For the next 30 days, I can follow through at the time we set." At the end of the 30 days, Ben hoped to talk about how it was working for both of them, and make any changes that might be necessary.

Ada nodded her approval. If Ben followed through, it should restore a meaningful connection. But if he failed, it would show that he couldn't keep his promises yet. To maintain his integrity in their relationship, he needed to grow into this new behavior.

Step 5: Positive Payoffs for Following Through

When a couple successfully keeps their commitments, healing and growth can take place for each partner. The gift of new words and actions can begin to heal lifelong hurts. The more they practice their new and positive ways of relating, the more they'll reinforce them.

By setting times to talk in a structured way, Ada and Ben's healing could take place on two levels. He could demonstrate that he cared enough to listen to her, and she could heal her old pain of feeling abandoned by the very people she had depended upon. Ben acknowledged that the new behavior pattern was going to be difficult, but by developing it, the two of them could reconnect and experience a deeper level of intimacy, or as some have called it, "into-me-see."

After time, with our support, couples commit to giving each other what they want. But when challenges surface outside our office and we're not there to help, partners often revert to the same old hurtful, reactive behaviors and get stuck.

That's why we make sure that each partner knows the positive payoffs in this process. Both Ada and Ben needed to stay motivated and follow through to their new way of relating.

To deepen Ben's understanding and empathy, Jesse asked Ada to "Tell him what receiving his gift will begin to heal in you."

Ada was very aware of the impact. "It will heal my core fear of abandonment and of not feeling important, and I'll begin to feel closer to you."

Ben needed to replace his behavior of withdrawing, criticizing, and breaking his promises when he felt vulnerable, smothered, or attacked. He needed to become more available to Ada, a relationship skill he'd been missing up until now. The MFG process can't be complete until one partner makes three requests and the other agrees to one of them—willingly and consistently. Otherwise, the gesture can't perform its healing effect. The receiving partner must show appreciation—positive recognition of their partner's willingness—in order to help motivate the partner to keep on freely giving it.

It's important for couples to go through all five steps in each other's presence, to let them "teach" each other about their internal process. After Ada was through, it was Ben's turn to share his side of their conflict.

Why did he withdraw when she criticized him and raised her voice? It was important that they both understand the reason behind his reactive behavior.

The Other Side of the Story

To discover his true feelings and desires, Ben made three requests—specific behaviors that Ada could perform to make him feel more cared about. By granting one of the three, she could understand him better and deepen their connection.

Beneath his withdrawal, Ben learned, was the experience of feeling over-whelmed and unheard in his childhood. Like Ada's father, Ben's dad had abandoned his family, leaving his wife to raise their eight children by herself. Growing extremely depressed, his mother forced 12-year-old Ben to take care of his brothers and sisters, do household chores, and prepare meals. Overwhelmed by so much adult responsibility, Ben couldn't participate in sports or extracurricular activities. On the rare occasions when he tried to talk about his feelings, his mother complained that he wasn't being sensitive to *her* needs and those of the family. To keep himself safe, he withdrew emotionally and sometimes physically. He held his pain and anger inside, not talking about his feelings to her or anyone else.

Ben (like Ada) wanted his mother to listen to him. And now he wanted Ada to hear him, especially when he felt overwhelmed. Because she was more assertive in initiating conversations about herself, Ben often felt left out, but feared that she might criticize him for changing the focus—just as his mother used to do.

Wanting an equal chance to be listened to, he made three requests of Ada. The one she chose to honor was to alternate their daily 15-minute *check-in's*, allowing each of them the same amount of time to be heard.

After each had explained their respective interpretations of the shared conflict, we reminded them that there are two sides to every story. Everyone has his own "reality" and "facts" about how conflicts arise and how to resolve them. So each partner must be willing to step into the other's reality. When each acknowledges the other's "take" on the situation, each feels better understood and more prepared to explore mutually satisfying solu-tions. But until each partner respects the other's reality, both will remain deadlocked in their ongoing power struggle, with each striving to be right and prove the other wrong.

Conflict as Opportunity

When both partners follow through on the specific behaviors they've committed to, they get the message that each is truly loved and cared about, and their relationship becomes peaceful and more fulfilling.

By taking the steps outlined above, any couple can gain a clearer view of what's really going on beneath the all-too-obvious surface. If you wonder if you're stuck with the wrong person because they constantly frustrate you, first identify your role in perpetuating the mutual nightmare. You may learn that it is possible to change your responses and help diffuse the situation.

Conflict lets you examine how you function in loving relationships, and how reactivity affects you in negative ways. The MFG process helps you see more clearly what you want, why you want it, and how you want to get it.

But it's so much simpler to blame your partner than to be honest about your own role in creating an impasse. Every step of the MFG process may prove difficult, and sometimes embarrassing. It is not easy to admit how you've hurt your beloved. Tracing your coping mechanisms and reactivity back to earlier painful relationships—and reliving childhood experiences—may make you feel disloyal to your childhood caregivers. You may be reluctant to talk about those earlier memories and may prefer to "let sleeping dogs lie." But feelings we don't acknowledge always haunt us the most.

If we can acknowledge painful feelings instead of disowning or ignoring them, they'll lose their power to poison our current—and future—relationships.

If It's so Hard, Why Bother?

When couples don't know how to get beyond the conflicts that keep them immobilized—and they tire of the arguments that interfere with the love they want from their partners—we encourage them to undertake the MFG process. Most couples are like Ada and Ben, sharing fond memories of when their love flowed freely. They want to re-experience those good feelings—and they can! If both practice MFG sincerely, it can help them actually dissolve past wounds. Then the root of conflict simply withers away—and each learns how to give and receive the love they both long for.

MFG is not about negotiation or compromise. Neither party has to give in or give up anything—except the pains of a lifetime. Once we have a tool for communicating our frustrations, we regain the deeper feelings of intimacy experienced during the romantic stage of our relationships. The more couples use MFG, the deeper the connection between them grows. Are their efforts worth it? Absolutely!

The high divorce rate is one indication of how many couples fail to resolve conflicts. People find a lifetime partner, but then they become mired in unresolved squabbles. Those who don't go their separate ways may remain filled with emotionally draining anger and helpless despair. Either way, the relationship is undermined.

Without exploring the emotions that fuel present conflicts, we lose the opportunity to heal past wounds. And we miss a chance to develop important relationship skills. Why continue to feel conflicted when you can spend more time feeling loved? Frustrating behavior uses up energy that could otherwise be used to dissolve conflicts and recreate the passion experienced in new romantic relationships.

Seven Couples Who Went Through the Five Steps

They came from many walks of life and from different age groups, races, and ethnic backgrounds. They had different interests, temperaments, and challenges. But each couple participated in an intensive 22-hour weekend seminar with us, to learn the basic tools for what many described as "deepening intimacy." Some followed up with private personal coaching.

For over a year, they met once a month in a follow-up support group and shared their personal stories. We learned a great deal about each couple's history and came to appreciate each individual's story and as well as their challenges, hopes, and relationship plans.

Yes, at times they still frustrate each other! But they manage their reactivity quite differently, and spend more time listening to each other than ever before. They spend considerably more time enjoying each other and far less time in conflict.

Every time they complete these five steps, they feel closer, having dissolved conflict. Each partner gets what he or she has always wanted—a feeling of restored connection that provides emotional nurturing and personal support.

They agreed to let us share their challenges so that others might relate to them and gain insight into their own relationships.

CHAPTER 3
THE 10 MOST COMMON RELATIONSHIP PROBLEMS

Every couple has their own unique set of personal and interpersonal problems. But over our nearly 60 years of combined clinical practice, we've identified the top ten relationship problems shared by couples, and listed them according to how often we've heard the complaint:

1. Communication

Many couples complain that their partners just don't listen to them. But few of us have been taught how to communicate successfully. If one of the two doesn't feel heard, communication breaks down and meaningful discussions leading to mutually satisfying decision-making can't take place. If either one shuts down and withdraws, or becomes reactive—yells, screams, or throws things—that behavior contributes to the communication breakdown. Problems aren't solved while fighting, fleeing, hiding, or simply surrendering to the other person's point of view. Couples may feel inclined to communicate less and less in order to cope, but it only exacerbates the problem. But with proper training, most couples can learn to communicate so that each feels understood and the problems of both can be resolved.

2. Blame and Criticism

Too many arguments begin because one partner gets upset and starts to blame and criticize the other, who then responds defensively. The confrontation escalates until one storms out of the room, leaving both feeling sad, angry, and victimized. To avoid the no-win "blame game" (which, if left unchecked can undermine the foundation of any relationship) couples need to learn the kinds of problem-solving tools that can transform potential arguments into meaningful dialogs.

3. Irreconcilable Differences

We're all different—thank God! That's what attracts us to each other. Each brings something different to an intimate relationship. Using these differences constructively, rather than letting them fuel irreconcilable disagreements, is the challenge.

Couples don't need to reconcile their differences, only their different*ness*. To succeed, each needs to honor the unique skills and perspectives of the other. But to do that, they may need professional help—especially if they've been deadlocked and fighting for a while. They must also improve their communication skills so that they can empathize with each other's ways. A more satisfying relationship requires new problem-solving skills to create mutually satisfying solutions, and this doesn't happen overnight. But with perseverance, even those "irreconcilable" differences can be replaced with cooperation, agreement, and love.

Which partner should take responsibility for getting things done? Our general rule is that it should be whoever's best at it. For example, if one partner is more adept at managing money, they should begin balancing the joint checking account.

But simple questions of who's better at child rearing or bargain shopping can present a challenge because the underlying question—who has the power and who's in control—prevents many couples from sharing their natural talents. Each person has a preferred way of doing things that's neither right nor wrong. But many demand that their way be the "only" way and that their partner must conform.

Rather than fight over it, it is healthier to find creative ways to honor each of your individual preferences.

4. Loss of Sexual Intimacy/Romance

New couples expect that the heightened intimacy of their early relationship will last forever. But unfortunately, lovemaking often gives way to the demands of managing two lives and eventually, a family. It's difficult to feel passionate when you're exhausted; and when the sex begins to wane, one or both may feel deceived.

Men may have an especially hard time understanding this loss of intensity because they remember how sexually active their partners were in the beginning. For women, there are many reasons for the loss of sexual excitement. For example, many feel that their men don't fully participate in managing the household. Far too often, she is trying to prepare dinner while he reads the paper or watches TV, asking, "When will dinner be ready?" If either partner is unhappy or resentful of the other, is it any wonder they don't enjoy an active sex life?

Despite all the strains of daily living, couples must make their relationship a priority or it will suffer. In school we are not usually taught how to successfully communicate and resolve problems. But we can learn from professionals who specialize in relationship dynamics. We strongly recommend that couples engage the help of books, classes, or a therapist/coach. Any combination of successful approaches can go a long way toward restoring the passion in our relationships.

Just as a plant needs water, light, and warmth to flourish, a relationship needs affection and nurturing to grow. Couples must plan time for fun and for romantic and intimate interaction.

5. Financial Problems

Many couples face loss of employment, lack money-management skills, or fall prey to the overuse of credit cards. Child support and alimony siphon away money from newly blended families—often spawning arguments across bloodlines over who decides how to spend what's left. When financial problems dominate, partners may become fearful about their future, affording them little space for relaxation and romance.

We've seen some couples who completely ignore the threat of financial issues. In other cases, one partner is willing to face the situation and starts to make independent financial plans, leading to a loss of trust and a serious breach in the relationship.

6. Time

Everyone is given the same 24-hour day, but some spend a disproportionate amount of time on unimportant things, throwing their lives out of balance.

When your relationship goes well, other things seem to work better too. But if not, everyone else pays the price for your unhappiness. Your relationship has to be at the very top of your priorities—even above child rearing, because one of the best things we can do for children is to show them parents who love and respect each other. When we first blended our family together, both of us were working demanding jobs. Eventually we realized that we were giving everything else more attention than we gave ourselves. We were not spending enough time with each other and with our sons.

So we scheduled time together, at least once a week, including weekend getaways and vacations. And we kept those appointments as faithfully as any others. We also made sure we scheduled time for our children. If someone wanted us during those scheduled times, we'd simply say, "Sorry, I have an appointment." We recommend that couples create a weekly "date night" when one comes up with a plan for what they will do together. Choices are alternated, so that each week the other partner gets to decide.

Remember that you are the foundation of your family. Everything else revolves around your devoting time to your relationship. Do so, or it will gradually erode, collapsing the family's unity along with it.

7. Built Up Resentments

Few couples were ever trained in the process of resolving problems. As a result, half of all first-time marriages end in divorce or separation, and many who stay together are unhappy.

When couples remain unable to resolve their differences, they need time and practice—training, then coaching—to work toward mutually satisfying solutions. Before they get to that point and seek solutions, one or both have just about given up. Some who have ended their relationships encourage other couples to "get help before you can no longer stand being in the same room." Why don't they? Usually, the unwilling partner offers a multitude of excuses, refusing to grasp how serious things are, no matter how the other partner tries to get through to them. In a breakup, emotional and financial costs can be devastating—for children as well as their parents, and those consequences often make one partner hesitate to admit that there is a problem.

But putting time and money into your relationship is the wisest investment you can make. And it's easy to find professionally trained psychotherapists who specialize in couples/marriage/partnership therapy. They advertise on the Internet and in the Yellow Pages, and recommendations can be found by word of mouth from those who've had good experiences.

Increasing numbers of children are living in one-parent households. If you are already having problems communicating, things will only intensify after you're married. We urge fiancés to learn communication and problem-solving skills before they say, "I do."

We find it amazing that a couple will spend thousands of dollars on their ceremony and reception, yet won't invest a few hundred dollars on "marriage insurance," developing the skills necessary to get through rough patches and stay together. Fortunately, more premarital couples are seeking help. Those who do so before entering marriage later say that they consider it one of the smartest things they've ever done.

8. Reluctance to Relinquish Past Mistakes

Nothing drains positive, loving energy faster than an unwillingness to forgive or forget—especially if partners are constantly reminded of their shortcomings. We're not condoning bad decision-making; but success is based on the ability to act on good decisions and learn from the bad ones. A partner who errs in judgment should be allowed to chart a new course without being constantly harangued. Rather than reminding your partner about a mistake, it's much more productive to talk over new options together and decide on a fresh course of action. When that produces successful results, you can celebrate that accomplishment together.

9. Affairs

Contrary to popular belief, infidelity doesn't have to mean the end of a relationship. Many who broke it off at the first sign of an affair regret having acted so hastily. The affair can be a wake-up call, indicating that a troubled relationship needs immediate attention in order to survive. Thousands of couples work through their pain to build more stable, mutually satisfying partnerships. They learn communications and problem-solving skills to help them better meet each other's needs and desires. In the long run, their relationships become even better than before. Yes, it takes time and perseverance, but the hard work pays off.

The one-time affair is far easier to overcome than infidelity with numerous partners. A serial cheater who continually engages in sexual exploits is far more difficult to trust. At some point, the faithful partner just gives up.

Those who find it difficult to remain faithful may suffer from a form of sexual addiction that can be overcome with consistent professional help. Addictive behaviors don't have to involve an actual relationship. Telephone sex, Internet porn sites and chat rooms, and XXX videos—none of which is necessarily harmful—can all lead to excessive indulgence. And when an individual prefers those kinds of sexual gratification, there's a problem that both partners need to address.

To repair the relationship, it's essential that the unfaithful party understand the depths of their partner's humiliation and feelings of betrayal. Straying partners shouldn't try to justify their behavior, minimize the impact it has, or blame anyone else for their actions. Only by understanding and having compassion for your partner's pain can you both begin to rebuild your relationship.

10. Children

Unfortunately many parents are unprepared for the tremendous responsibilities of parenthood. It's crucial that couples anticipate the impact that a child will have on their relationship. Beginning with the infant's first cry for attention, parents are on call 24-7, with the baby's constant needs often becoming a major source of couple conflict.

The parents may feel trapped. Before long, tempers flair and arguments ensue. Often, the new mother is so overly protective that she's unwilling to leave her infant's care to anyone else. Individual needs often take a back seat to the child's, and many parents feel they must compete for their partner's attention. They start to feel guilt over their resentful, conflicted emotions. Family and close friends can provide a much- needed break for couples to help them nurture the relationship and create special times together that both need.

Why Does MFG Work so Well?

Because couples learn two important things: 1) the underlying reasons for their frustrations and 2) very specific tools for overcoming the behaviors that fuel those frustrations.

At the heart of their problems is the disconnection that each partner feels when things don't go well. Through MFG, couples learn how to create a safe emotional space for themselves. They begin to listen and hear each other fully and make sense out of what the other person is saying. Once partners achieve this insightful compassion for each other, healing, growth and transformation can begin.

The goal is to not merely solve, but *dissolve* problems, by restoring a lost sense of connection. And as parents help each other evolve to a greater level of maturity, they can become better role models for their children.

As you'll see in the final "case history" of this book, we've had to do the same MFG work that we facilitate for our clients. When our own frustrations surface, these tools and processes help us forestall what could otherwise grow into major conflicts. MFG helps us both stay on track. We now feel comfortable with this process. Like so many others—including our clients—have discovered, the strong commitment to the effort is well worth it in terms of the payoff gained by transforming your relationship with your beloved!

CHAPTER 4
BUDDY AND SOPHIE'S STORY
FINANCIAL PROBLEMS

"Behind the Closed Doors of an All-American Family"

This is the story of an "ideal" American family—a husband, a wife, and two gifted, talented, high achieving children—a boy and a girl. They lived in a lovely home in an upscale community and had a playful and loyal dog. On the outside, everything looked perfect. But like so many other families, they had been experiencing incredible conflict, disconnection, and pain behind the proverbial white picket fence.

But Buddy and Sophie were fortunate enough to rediscover the deep love, caring, and respect they had for each other. Their story is about a journey home again, back to a place where they made a real reconnection. They were willing to share it so that others might be inspired to learn the steps they took toward healing their relationship.

Sophie and Buddy, a Jewish couple in their forties, had been married for fourteen years. When we first met Buddy, he impressed us as a clean-cut fellow with a kind demeanor and a great sense of humor. He had deep-set hazel eyes behind wire-rimmed glasses and sometimes wore a baseball cap to hide his receding hairline. Self-employed as a home improvement consultant, he was fully involved with their two children. Sophie said that one of the first things she noticed about Buddy was "his friendly smile" She said he was comfortable-looking. "You can tell he was athletic when he was younger," she added, "and that the years have caught up with his midsection."

Sophie has short curly hair and a warm, round face with a dimple on her upper left cheek. Buddy says that Sophie "has the kind of energy that makes her stand out in a crowd". The first thing people notice about her is her beautiful green eyes, robust smile, and a hearty and instantly recognizable laugh. Sophie worked full-time as an attorney, but was also a fully involved mom. Both parents actively supported their children's academic, social, and recreational activities.

"When I met Sophie," Buddy said, "I wasn't thinking about emotional intimacy. I was thinking about sexual intimacy." At the time, she was an attractive 17 and he was 20. She was dating a close friend of his, who kept urging him to ask Sophie out. So finally he did. When she first met Buddy, Sophie recalls, they were part of a group of friends who simply hung out. "We all went out and had long talks. Somehow I always seemed to be talking to Buddy at end of the night. I just thought he was really interesting, really smart, funny, and fun to be with.

"Then Buddy asked me out. Initially I refused because I wasn't at all physically attracted to him. But the group kept going out together, and we always wound up talking at the end of the night. I began to see qualities in Buddy beyond his physique." Over time, something changed. He continued to be fun to be with, and became even more interesting. "I learned that he really was a genius and was intellectually stimulating. As time progressed, he even became more physically attractive." New feelings surfaced: "I was ready to begin dating him."

"When we started dating," she added, "I guess there just wasn't a whole lot of thought process to it. It was like, 'Okay, now we date,' and we kept dating. At first it was very romantic—forbidden and everything! I hid our dating from my parents, because I was dating an older man. I was seventeen, remember, and he was twenty."

They dated for about five years. "When we finished college and I began to launch my career," Sophie recalls, "I said to him 'Hey, Buddy, I'm ready to get married.'

"Basically, the proposal was about as romantic as that. We just had good times. We always just had fun and enjoyed being together. We could talk about problems he had with his brothers, my difficulties with my parents, and all that. We tried to help each other solve those problems. I always felt really comfortable with Buddy."

They married in 1983. Three years later Sophie began law school, which consumed her life for the next four years. Buddy recalled how "Those years went by so fast they felt like six months. She was taking classes and I was taking classes. We had totally different schedules, but when we finally got time to spend together, we had fun. And wound up in bed." Sophie concurred: "Yeah, since we barely ever saw each other, it was pretty exciting when we actually got together. When I wasn't studying, or away, we'd go out. We went out a lot, and it was fun."

They recall that for about five years, it was like great dating. The feelings weren't super-intense; they had already settled down and felt comfortable and familiar. But things were fine. They had great summers, vacations, and lingering romantic weekends.

Then, in the sixth year, they had a child. And yes, as you might have guessed, things began to shift in a different direction.

From Romance to Frustration

After their wedding, and before their first child was born, there were isolated incidents of expressed frustrations. They would fight, but it wouldn't feel like they were really in a power struggle. "It was just like, 'Okay, people have their fights. Just move on and don't worry about addressing the issues.' " Sophie said.

"Yeah," Buddy recalls. "In the beginning she would call me a pack rat because I didn't throw anything away."

"That's right," responded Sophie. "It didn't bother me so much in the beginning, because I was so busy studying for law school. I might say something about it from time to time and then let it go. I thought he would change."

Shortly after Sophie graduated, their first child was born. "Then," they both said in unison, "everything changed." They had less time for fun and play, since they had to work, find day care, and tackle responsibilities at home. Soon after, Buddy was laid off from his job. He tried hard to find full-time work, with no success, then started a painting business, which brought in little money. He had ideas for increasing their income but didn't feel that Sophie was supportive because she didn't think his ideas were workable. With his reduced income, they began to depend upon Sophie to maintain their family's lifestyle. Buddy grew depressed, but didn't share his feelings with Sophie. She felt drained from a long commute, a stressful job, and coming home to household responsibilities. When she began putting pressure on Buddy to bring in more money, he became even more depressed. This became the foundation for their fights.

After about four years of repeating the same arguments—and one year before her 40th birthday—Sophie felt so overwhelmed and burdened with responsibilities that she decided she needed some relief. She felt that she was being used by Buddy and got to a point where she had had enough. Reluctantly, she decided to file for divorce and felt ready to tell their children she wanted their father to move out.

When they realized how devastating divorce might be for them and the children, they elected to come to us for counseling, but Sophie only agreed to go to the first session. During that session, she began to learn more about Buddy's internal struggles and decided to put the divorce on hold. Then Buddy and Sophie began exploring the issues at the root of their conflicts.

Sophie knew she had two core frustrations. The first was the financial pressures she was experiencing by providing the primary source of income for the family. Her second was Buddy's tendency to be a packrat, leaving her with the chore of cleaning up after him. The financial problem was a lot more difficult for Sophie than cleaning the house. Because it was easier, clearing and cleaning up after Buddy is where she put her attention.

Because home wasn't restful and created anxiety for Sophie, she would awaken two or three hours before Buddy. As soon as she got up, she became aware of how she couldn't stand the mess in their house. So she decided what needed to be kept and what didn't and she began throwing things out. By the time Buddy got up, her frustrations and resentments had intensified to the point that she approached him coldly and started barking out orders. "The way I reacted when I got to this level of anger was to stop talking to Buddy, but I wouldn't tell him why," she said.

At first, Buddy didn't notice that she'd stopped talking to him, until he became aware that he was missing one or more of his magazines. "I'd go looking for them because I knew they'd be there. Then all of a sudden they were gone. I'd panic and spend hours tearing things apart searching for them. I'd be mad. I would just boil and boil, slam doors, pound on tables, and swear."

"You'd call me at work." Sophie added, and say "Where did you put my stuff?" She would often be in a meeting and would tell him to leave a message on her voice mail.

"This," Buddy said, "would get me madder and even more frustrated."

Sophie: "When he couldn't find what he was looking for, he would become so resentful."

"I'd shut down," he said. "I would withdraw from Sophie and go into hibernation. I wouldn't say anything and wouldn't do anything. I just didn't want to deal with her or the frustration. I think what bothered me the most was how she expressed her frustration with me. Usually it was with a criticism or she would start barking orders. I just shut down."

Sophie said that when she couldn't make any progress with Buddy she would escape into her work. In work she found order and organization and she could distract herself from anxiety.

Sophie: "We didn't deal with our frustrations with big fights or yelling. We did the Cold War sort of thing. I gave looks; he'd slam. Or I'd just decide that I was too tired and I'd go to bed. I can't tell you the number of times I've gone to bed because I didn't want to deal with something."

They felt stuck.

After sharing our ideas about the dynamics we observed, the couple realized that their reactions to each other's frustrating behaviors were probably at the surface level of an ongoing deeper conflict. They decided to explore below the surface, and

Sophie went first.

Sophie Describes The Frustrating Behavior That Triggers Her

Jesse asked Sophie to take a moment and identify the specific behavior of Buddy that triggers her. While this step seems simple enough, it is challenging for some people because they are aware that they're emotionally upset but may have trouble pinpointing and articulating the specific behavior associated with their upset. After Sophie got in touch with that behavior, Melva asked her to turn and face Buddy and describe it.

She slowly turned and said, "Buddy, what frustrates me is that you are not being an equal contributing partner in our household finances. I feel responsible for everything and I'm overwhelmed. I worry about what will happen to us if I should ever get sick and not am able to work. How will we live? I believe that you can do more but you're not. I'm frustrated."

Buddy was clearly upset by what Sophie said and wanted to respond. "I've got something I've got to say," he said, but we told him to just listen to what Sophie was saying because it was important that she felt she was being heard. When Buddy calmed down, we asked him to repeat back to Sophie what she has said, and he did a good job of that.

Sophie Identifies Her Emotional Feelings and Reactive Behavior

Jesse asked Sophie to share with Buddy what she feels when he is not being an equal financial partner in the relationship. She turned to him and said

"Often, I am scared but I try hard not to go there. So I cover that feeling by being frustrated. Then I get angry and that leads to resentment. Then I get depressed. So I have a range of feelings—fear, frustration, anger, resentment, and depression. I really try to explain my feelings to you but in spite of what I say or how I say it you just don't get it. That makes me even more frustrated. Then, you make it worse by getting angry at me for bringing it up. So I respond by being cold and emotionally distant. Then I start making demands. I am not a pleasant person to be with."

While she may have felt justified, her reactions did not contribute to solving the problem, and Sophie had just verbally clarified her role in perpetuating the conflict.

Digging Deeper Beneath The Surface

What hurt lay below her anger? we asked. "What hurts…" Sophie started to answer but then paused and began asking us questions. Melva suggested that she direct those questions to Buddy, and she did: "Why can't you hear me? Why can't you understand what I'm trying so hard to get across? If you know what I need, why don't you just give it to me?"

Jesse asked her to pause and take a few deep breaths, and then posed the question again: "What hurts about Buddy not getting it?"

"Oh," she said, and thought for a few moments. "I guess the other part that hurts is that I feel so used when I have to take care of so many responsibilities."

She had just excavated a deeper layer of feelings.

"What fear lies below the hurt?"

Sophie probed within herself. "My fear is of being used."

Sophie Connects Her Childhood History To Her Current Needs

Sophie grew up in a house filled with chaos. Most of the time, there were expressions of anger, along with physical and emotional abuse. She was raised by a mother who was diagnosed as bipolar and a father who was a Holocaust survivor.

"Because of my mom's problems, she wasn't able to be 'the adult' a lot of times. When I went to her for advice, I'd end up comforting and taking care of her. That was when I first began to feel used. I mean, she would occasionally come up with some sort of advice, but it was like a 'pat' answer she had read in some women's magazine. She couldn't connect it with who I was, and she's still like that. You can't really talk to her about things, because she will say what she thinks people are supposed to say." Sophie thought that her fear of being used had some clear connections to those childhood experiences.

Buddy added, "Talking to her mother is like watching something like 'Leave It to Beaver' on TV. With her, everything is scripted."

"Yeah, "Sophie chimed in, "not connected to real experience. So many times I felt used, having to take on a lot of adult responsibilities at a young age, like my parents giving me the responsibility for parenting my brother. So with Buddy, I feel I'm doing more than my share—when I don't really feel he's taking his share of the responsibilities, be it the house, the kids, finances, whatever. When I feel like I'm being used, that's a real big trigger for me."

We knew this was the time when Sophie could learn what she needed to help heal those wounds from her past.

Sophie Identifies Her Wants and Desires

Melva asked Sophie what she needed in the past that she hadn't gotten. Immediately she said, "I really wanted my mother to pay attention to what was going on with me. I wanted her to take care of me emotionally, instead of me taking care of her." She began to cry quietly. "It wasn't fair. I felt so alone!"

She continues to cry quietly while sharing the pain of what her childhood experience was like, and Buddy reached out to comfort her. She had just identified the first gold nugget of the MFG process, and because their connection was so tender, we decide to give the couple time to savor their feelings.

We ended the session by giving Sophie homework to help her bring her desires into focus. She and Buddy agreed to return the following week and then left, hand in hand.

When they returned, they reported having several moments of conflict. After having enjoyed such a positive, connecting session, they couldn't understand why it happened. How could they feel so close to each other during the session, and then encounter such difficulties only two days later? We explained that whenever couples experience such intense connection, they need time to integrate those good feelings. It helps to take a short break from each other so that the positive feelings of reconnection can settle in. Conflict helps provide that break. Many couples don't know this, so we generally alert them to anticipate it.

Making an Outrageous Request

Jesse asked Sophie to share her next two gold nuggets with Buddy—her global and specific desires. We asked her to imagine herself in a candy store, where she could have anything she wanted. What would that be? She pondered for a few minutes and said, "Even though I had a week to think about this, it was difficult. I usually don't think about what I want. So you want me to be in a candy store; let's see, being in a candy store. Hmmm . . . I got it! If I could have anything, I'd want Buddy to always earn enough money and hire all the staff we would need to be completely responsible for all our finances and manage the cooking, cleaning, kids, and everything else." Both of them laugh. Buddy said, "I like that too!"

A More Realistic Request

Sophie then put her desire into more realistic terms. "I want you to take your business more seriously so that it starts making enough money for you to be a full partner with me in our household finances. And if you need help from me, I want you to communicate it clearly so that I can get an accurate picture of what help you need." Buddy nodded, indicating that he understood.

Sophie Makes Three Specific Behavioral Requests

Now Sophie was to make three specific requests of Buddy, including new behaviors that he could give to her to replace the frustrating behavior that triggered her emotional disconnection. Sophie found this step somewhat frustrating. "Already it's difficult to think about what I want. It's even harder to describe what I want, specifically. Is it okay if I take another week to think about this?" We agreed.

Sophie worked on her homework and prepared her requests for the following session. We reminded her to make her requests specific, behavioral, measurable, and positive.

"Buddy, once a week for the next four weeks, for a minimum of 30 minutes each session, I want you to sit down with me and share your ideas about the business so that I know and understand what your business goals and plans are." Buddy repeated it back to Sophie and she acknowledged. Sophie's second request was that "Once a week for the next 90 days for one hour per session, I want us to review the income and expenses of the business and make plans to increase profits." Again, Buddy repeated what he had heard.

"My third request is that within the next two weeks, I would like for you to tell me specifically what I can realistically do to make our business more successful." Buddy repeats her third request.

Buddy grimaced as he ranked each request as being easy, hard, or extremely hard. Each one was hard, he said, because when they made commitments to follow through on things something often came up, generally something to do with their kids. But he agreed to do his part. "Okay", he said, "I choose number three as well as number two. I understand that it is important that you know about what is happening with our business and that you want us to work together to make it successful. You have a need to be part of a team and to feel supported so you don't have to take responsibility for everything. I love you and I care about what you need." Melva encouraged him to commit to one and give the others as a surprise. "I can do that," he said with a smile.

Sophie was deeply moved. They looked at each other lovingly, embraced, and gave each other a tender kiss.

We wanted them to take a few moments to savor this memorable experience. After a few moments more, we told them that they had more work to do.

Identifying the Positive Payoffs for Each Partner

We knew there would be significant advantages if Sophie and Buddy followed through on these requests. But they also needed to figure out for themselves what those payoffs would be.

Jesse asked Sophie, "What healing will occur for you when Buddy grants your requests?" We assigned her the task of thinking about it and coming the next week prepared to share her insights with Buddy. His homework was to prepare to share with Sophie the particular relationship skill he thought he would develop if he followed through on her requests.

The following week, Sophie reported that "It wasn't easy because I normally don't think about getting benefits from other people. Not getting what I want and need from those important to me has become what I expect. She had written something to share with Buddy, and turned toward him and said "Receiving this gift from you will help me heal the pain of feeling that I have to take responsibility for everybody and everything. I will feel that the two of us would be solving a problem together. Instead of feeling used, I'll feel supported, taken care of, and hopeful about our future."

Next, it was Buddy's turn. Buddy also reported a positive payoff. "Participating together in discussing and planning our business goals will help me feel that I am also supported. I'll feel more respected and better about myself."

He admitted that his internal experience of giving Sophie this gift would be difficult. "When I was growing up, I didn't get support when I needed it. It makes sense that it's hard to give to another person something that I haven't experienced myself. But I'm learning that I need help in very specific areas, and so does Sophie. Now I know this is a priority for her. I know that it will make an important difference for her." Buddy committed himself to doing his part in following through on Sophie's requests. "I can really live with the fact that this new behavior is hard for you, "Sophie said. "You're telling me that you're having a difficult time—but this works better for me than you clamming up or pounding on tables!"

Buddy's Story: The Same Situation, Different Reality

Buddy Describes the Surface of the Conflict from His Perspective

Each person in a relationship has her or his own experience of the situation when they have been triggered and are deep into the conflict. We explored Sophie's experience and learned a great deal about her internal world. Sophie and Buddy were made aware of what triggered her and of her past childhood history that contributed to unmet needs, desires, and longings. Buddy heard Sophie "with new ears" and reached out to her with understanding and empathy. They agreed to practice some new behaviors and identified the positive payoffs. The MFG process has already proven to be extremely helpful to Buddy and Sophie, and we are only halfway through the process.

Melva asked Buddy to finish this sentence; "Sophie, when you..." He paused for a moment and then said, "Sophie, when you get upset with me over our finances and either withdraw from me emotionally, become cold and distant and don't talk to me, or start barking out orders and making demands, it's really hard for me. I don't think you realize how much I am impacted by it. I try my best for it not to bother me but it does. I feel awful. I don't believe that I can live up to your expectations, that I can provide for you and our family, that you can feel financially secure with me, or that I can make you happy. So I feel inadequate, my self esteem is in the toilet because I just don't feel that I am capable of being the person I want to be as your husband, as a man, and as your partner."

Jesse asked Sophie to repeat back to Buddy what she has heard him say. As she began to speak, Buddy became tearful. Buddy had tapped into deeper feelings and just hearing Sophie repeat back to him his emotional pain touched him deeply. Sophie also became teary eyed and reached out to touch his hand.

"And so Buddy, what do you do when Sophie becomes distant or starts to bark out orders?" Melva asked.

"First I get angry. Then I withdraw and hibernate. And then, I get really, really depressed."

Buddy Digs for His Underlying Feelings

Jesse asked, "What's hurting you when you get so depressed?" He hung his head, looked at Sophie, and paused.

"What hurts me most is that I feel so terribly inadequate as a person, a

husband, a father, and a provider. And while I am in that state, Sophie withdraws from me so I feel so alone in my grief and pain. There is no one there to reassure me that I am okay, to tell me that they believe in me, that I can achieve success if I keep working at the business and get the kind of help and support I need to make it profitable. I really want to be able to provide my family with the kind of financial security that they deserve. But when you withdraw from me, Sophie, I feel so alone and totally hopeless. I go deeper and deeper into my depression and I have no one to comfort or reassure me. It's awful. I feel like a complete failure." He began to cry almost uncontrollably.

Even though Buddy shared many of his internal thoughts and feelings, we knew there were likely to be even more emotional feelings underneath. Generally, men in our society have been socialized to not express emotional feelings, and we wanted to take advantage of this opportunity for Buddy to get in touch with and to express as many of his feelings as possible. This would be of benefit to both Buddy and Sophie. From our experience, there is usually fear beneath the surface that needs to be explored.

After a while Buddy regained his composure. We waited for a few minutes while he allowed himself to be with his feelings, and then asked him if we could continue. He said yes, and Melva asked, "What's the worst thing that could happen if you and Sophie continue to be so unhappy?"

"If things continue this way my fear is that Sophie will divorce me. She will leave me and will take our children and I will be left all alone feeling like a complete and total failure. The thought of that is unbearable. I can't imagine anything worse than that. I truly love Sophie and our children and I want our family to be together. I want to be the kind of husband and father that they all can look up to. I want to have the marriage and family for our kids that I didn't have when I was growing up. I know we can make it work if we both work at it and get the help we're receiving now."

Buddy Connects His Past to the Present

Jesse said, "Buddy, we really want to acknowledge you for getting in touch with and sharing your very painful feelings about this situation. This has required great personal insight and courage to go into those 'dark places' that many of us would rather avoid. We have been deeply touched by what you have shared. We better understand, respect, and feel closer to you than ever before and sincerely appreciate your allowing us to get to know these parts of you. And because you have been courageous enough to take these steps, we want you to know that you have begun your transformational process and we celebrate this accomplishment with you. You have talked about feeling inadequate, depressed, and alone when Sophie withdraws from you. We would like to know what those feelings remind you of...what are your earliest memories of feeling that way?"

Buddy responded by saying, "I can't see how any other past relationships have anything to do with the hurt and fears I am feeling with Sophie." Melva told him that his feelings made sense and that the origins of these feelings are likely to have had a history from his childhood.

Jesse asked if he was willing to explore a short guided imagery to trace possible memories relating to his current conflict with Sophie.

"I think I need to be with what I've done today before going deeper. I've gone deeper today than I could have imagined." We agreed with Buddy and acknowledged him for what he had accomplished. In preparation for our next appointment, we offered him a short questionnaire designed to support him in recalling his childhood past and making the connection to his current relationship with Sophie. Our agreement was that he would only use it if he felt okay about it, and Buddy agreed.

Sophie looked him lovingly in his eyes and said, "Buddy, you are not alone. I am here for you." They embraced and left the office arm in arm. A shift had occurred and we believed that they were about to embark upon a whole new relationship.

A week later, Sophie and Buddy were back. Buddy had completed most of the questionnaire. To his surprise, he had recalled a number of forgotten childhood memories. He said he was even more astonished that what hurt and scared him in the past was so similar to what was bothering him now.

"When I was growing up I felt abandoned and alone. My father abandoned me physically when he left the family and started a new life on his own. He left me with my mother and she abandoned me emotionally. Neither of them was really there for me, to support me or give me the encouragement that I wanted and needed to be successful in life. If I was to make it, I knew that I would have to do it on my own."

He sat up in his chair, holding a bottle of water tightly in his hand and said, "Man, this hurts! I didn't like those people." Buddy also connected the feeling of not being important with other childhood memories:

"Compared to my brothers, I felt like I was the least important to my mother. She seemed to mother everyone except me! She actually told me that I had to take a backseat to my older brother. Then along comes *little* brother, and all of her attention went to him. So my brothers received all of her praise and recognition. My only purpose in life was to support them. I got almost no help, no really meaningful support of any kind. Instead, what I got was a lot of criticism. I could never do things the way my mother wanted. So I felt inadequate, unimportant, insignificant, and incapable. I was also extremely depressed and felt alone a lot of the time. I have had these feelings for a long time and they get triggered when Sophie gets upset with me."

Sophie offered an insight of her own. "Recently I learned something about him that struck me very powerfully. Buddy told me about something that happened to him on numerous occasions as a little boy, long before his father left. He said that one time he came in from playing, and his mom was in the kitchen with a cup of coffee in one hand, a cigarette in the other, and the telephone on her shoulder. He tried to get her attention by yelling out 'Mom! Mom!' He was excited to tell her something. She replied, 'Go away, I'm busy, I'm on the phone' and brushed him away with the hand holding the cigarette. She burned him!"

"Yeah," Buddy added, "she used to *accidentally* burn me with her cigarettes. I had these big burns on my face and hands. My mother said it was because I put myself in the way, so it was my fault.

"She never did it deliberately," Buddy said quickly, "But she just never paid enough attention, or I wasn't important enough for her to prevent it. I mean, if this were happening today, teachers would report it and the authorities would be knocking on the door."

While we didn't believe that each time he got burned it was by accident, Buddy didn't appear to be ready to accept the idea that his mother burned him deliberately.

Sophie immediately rose from her chair, walked over to Buddy, and put her arms around him. This time tears were flowing from her eyes. She held him for a several minutes while whispering in his ear. It was a very tender moment so we allowed them the time they needed to experience it.

Buddy Identifies His Wants and Desires

What Buddy Wanted From His Mother

When we sensed the time was right, Melva asked Buddy to state what he wanted from his mother that he never got. He took a deep breath, sighed, and said tearfully, "All I really wanted from her was some attention along with maybe a little love, caring, support and encouragement. I wanted to feel that I was important to her and that she believed that I was talented and capable and in my own unique ways was a little different from my brothers." This was the first important gold nugget that Buddy uncovered.

What Buddy Wanted From Sophie

Sophie had been listening attentively and was emotionally moved as Buddy shared his painful memories. We asked Buddy, "What is it that you want from Sophie that you haven't been getting?"

Sophie turned toward Buddy. "Yes Buddy, what do you want and need from me? I want to know."

"I want a lot of the same things I wanted from my mother but never got", Buddy professed. I want, no, I need your help, your support, your ideas, your knowledge, and your encouragement, especially with the business. I want it to be successful so that I can be an equal partner with you in creating financial security for our family both now and in the future. You are already meeting my needs in so many other ways in our relationship, and I want you to know that."

Buddy Makes an Outrageous Request

Jesse asked Buddy to make an outrageous request of Sophie.

"Let me see. If I could have anything I wanted, it would be that you would never, ever, complain about anything about me again!"

They both broke into laughter. And while they both knew that such a request was extremely unlikely, they also knew that there was a part of Buddy that did seriously want Sophie to never again make a complaint about him.

Buddy Makes a More Realistic Request

Melva asked Buddy to make a more realistic request this time.

"Sophie, it's quite simple what I want and need from you. I really need your help, support and ideas with *our* business. I can't do it alone. I need help--not a whole lot of help so that you feel even more overwhelmed. Just a little help."

Buddy Makes Three Specific Requests of Sophie to Get the Help He Needs

"Buddy," Jesse said, "We want you to offer Sophie three specific ways that she can help you with the business. Your requests must be positive, specific, outline behavior that you want, and explain how many times and how often you want it. Do not use any negatives like 'stop,' 'quit,' or 'do not.' And do not use absolutes like 'always' or 'never.' The goal is to make three requests she is able to do that will enable you to have what you want from her. The more specific you can be, the better. Sophie will select one to give you as a gift—not because of a demand or obligation. So think about your three requests for getting the help you need."

After reflection, he came up with these:

"My first request is that for the next three months, once a week for an hour, we will have a meeting to review the status of the business and can make joint decisions about what to do to better support it. My second request is that for two hours per week for the next 60 days you will help me with the accounting, record keeping, organizing, and maintaining of our business files so I can be a better manager. And my third request is that once a week for the next six weeks, at a time that is mutually acceptable, you answer my legal questions and give me legal advice. In the home improvement business, there are legal issues that come up all the time and I need help to address them."

Sophie listened intently and repeated each request to make sure she had heard each one clearly.

Sophie Ranks Buddy's Requests

She said that his first request would be easy, his second would be hard because of the amount of time involved, and that the third would be especially hard because of her lack of experience in that aspect of law.

Sophie Chooses a Request to Offer Buddy as a Gift

Sophie said her desire would be to grant him all three of his requests but that realistically, she could only commit to the first one, but would think about ways to help him with the other two requests, if possible.

Identifying Positive Payoffs for each Partner

Buddy knew that Sophie's willingness to grant him his request would help heal the wounds he experienced during his conflict with her. What he didn't know was that it would also help heal his childhood wounds. The request also gave Sophie a payoff of growth.

She said, "Earlier in our marriage, before we had kids, I became very work-oriented. I worked a lot of hours and then went to law school at night. I was so busy I didn't realize that I had to put time into our relationship. I thought it would take care of itself on its own, but now I see that I will have to work at it. Also, I am aware that complaining, barking orders at Buddy or withdrawing does not solve the problem. The growth for me is to follow through on Buddy's request. This will enable me to take a positive, corrective, problem solving approach to addressing our issues. I'm sure that my old, automatic, reactive behavior patterns are likely to creep in every once and awhile. And, I am promising myself and Buddy that I am going to work hard at following through on his request and am open to exploring others that might make things better for us. I will be able to slow down, feel more relaxed, and there'll be less escalation of conflict between us."

Moving Through to a Restored Loving Connection

Sophie and Buddy had begun to restore an intimate emotional connection with each other. Sophie said, "I made that initial decision to file for divorce because the way things were going, I didn't see any hope for us. I didn't see any desire on Buddy's part to face the issues and work on our problems. But that's changed. We've *both* changed and are working on our relationship and having wonderful results."

Her eyes lit up, and Buddy smiled. Then he said, "I had no idea that we could get to this place. We've been working pretty hard at it for the past few years. There was a time when things were getting pretty bad. She started talking about something at work, and I'd say, 'You know, I don't want to listen to it. You aren't willing to listen to what I've got going on so I don't want to listen to you anymore.' I think that was like a door slamming. Then I got the divorce papers."

Sophie added, "Only now, when we're really past the danger of splitting up, our daughter makes little comments like, 'It really scares me when you and Daddy fight, because I think you're going to break up.' And a lot of times when we let our kids see us hugging and kissing, they'll go, 'Eew.' But the last couple of months, our daughter has been, like, 'Oh, do it again. I like it when you guys kiss. I like it!' "

Melva told Buddy and Sophie that if they had gotten divorced, as many people do, likely each of them would have found another partner who would frustrate them in the exact same way. They would probably react the same way and get stuck again and again. And there was a good chance that their next relationship would end the same way.

Buddy chimed in, "And we'd make the same mistakes all over again."

Sophie agreed. "Absolutely."

The frustration in our committed love relationships and our reactions to them, Jesse told them, would show up as the same lesson over and over again—as many times as needed for us to finally "get it." The lesson was that it's not only the other person who has to change. *We* ourselves must change in order to give and receive the quality of love that we desire and deserve.

Where Buddy and Sophie Are Now

Many couples need help in learning how to support each other emotionally. Buddy and Sophie's relationship is now growing in several ways, mainly because they have learned how to be mutually supportive. They're learning to make each other's needs a priority. Their experiences growing up didn't encourage them to ask their caretakers for what they wanted. But now they're learning to ask each other—and others—for what they want and are now having fun together again. Buddy said, "We talk about our feelings and hurts more. We're committed to improving our relationship. We're working hard on it because it's important to us, and now we've got a lot of factors working in our favor."

"You know," Sophie added, "I don't think I ever sat down and thought about what it means to be emotionally close to another person. I never asked myself, 'Do I really listen to him? Do I really understand his perspective? Or am I using him all the time, dumping my problems on him?' Is he the one who's not speaking up enough about what his perspective is, what his needs are? Back then, I didn't think I needed to learn anything about relationships. Did I ever have a lot to learn! And I'm still learning.

"We're the most intimate that we have ever been," she added. "It's more than either of us ever had, I think. Intimacy, for us, is being able to talk about any issue. We're at the stage where certain things can be just too explosive, too difficult, that we can't deal with them on our own. But we *know* that. For now, we stay away from trying to address those issues on our own, because our emotional connection is still very fragile. Melva is coaching us through the rough spots."

Buddy said, "I think Sophie's the only person I've ever really opened up to, because I've got a wall I've built that's big and wide and deep. She's tried walking around it, climbing over it, and busting through it. Eventually, she found a hole in it. But for me, it's the vulnerability thing, letting my blemishes hang out. And I'm starting to learn that it's an active thing, something you have to do to have a mutually satisfying relationship. There are no short-cuts."

CHAPTER 5
MICHAEL AND SIMONE'S STORY
AFFAIRS: REWRITING A FAIRY-TALE ROMANCE

"I paged you four times today. Why didn't you answer?" she said in anger.

"I told you. I was at the gym and didn't hear it. Since I didn't know that you paged until I was on my way home, I decided to wait until I got here. What's the problem?" Michael said, puzzled and frustrated.

Simone and Michael are an African American couple married 25 years. Their fairy tale romance began in their teens, when a strong attraction, followed by a deepening love, developed between them. To be certain, they have experienced many personal and relationship challenges—the kind that would drive most couples apart. But the continued strength of their bond has sustained them through those challenges.

Simone was a stunningly attractive woman of medium height with light brown, flawless skin and golden brown, full, curly, chic-styled hair. She had the kind of presence that caused people to pay attention when she entered a room. Warm and friendly, aware of her surroundings, and with a great sense of humor, she was able to help people relax and feel comfortable. She greeted them with enthusiasm and showed an interest in getting to know them.

When we met her she was a stay-at-home mom with the youngest of their three children and was exploring several creative writing projects. She was also learning how to play golf, her husband's favorite summer sport.

Michael was a handsome, soft-spoken man, also of medium height, with a smooth, milk chocolate skin tone and a debonair sense of style. He was well dressed, poised, dignified, bright, intelligent, aware, and attentive. He had a keen sense of humor and a somewhat laid-back demeanor. An executive for a major corporation, Michael was an avid golfer and an energetic basketball player.

The scenario described in the beginning of this story had been relived over and over during their 25-year marriage. For Simone it did not fit the happily-ever-after image she had envisioned when she married Michael; and it caused her to feel ignored. For Michael, it was an experience of not feeling trusted.

They got to that point gradually. Their romance began when a friend introduced Michael to Simone. He was eighteen; she was fourteen. "Instantly, the magic began," Simone said as her face lit up.

Michael smiled and they both laughed in an almost childlike way. "Meeting Simone was like meeting an angel. She was, without a doubt, the most beautiful woman I had ever met. I was instantly attracted to her."

Simone smiled and giggled. She tossed back her curly brown hair, heaved a big sigh, and added, "Meeting Michael was quite an extraordinary experience. He was always able to make me laugh, and I was flattered by the interest of an older boy. Whenever we were together, which wasn't often because of our age difference, the time was special." She thought for a moment, then continued. "I guess we were both elevated above the burdens we carried in our families, and we found a sense of joy and freedom we had not experienced before. We cherished every opportunity to be together. It was like running away to a place of our own. I felt like Cinderella and Michael felt like my Prince Charming. It was my fairy tale come to life."

Michael said what was special for him was that "It was the first time I had someone to talk about my problems with. As an adolescent, I had lots of problems I had to deal with on my own. I'd come home from school and sit in my chair. I would just sit there and try to figure out how to manage all my problems. I had to try to sort through it by myself. That's how I learned to survive. Simone was the first person I could really talk to about what was going on with me. She listened and didn't make me feel like I was weak or a failure of some kind. That was significant. It's odd that I only saw her as being carefree. I didn't realize that she was under the same kind of pressure to perform that I was. It wasn't evident to me in the beginning."

"With Simone," Michael continued, "I could remove the façade and become vulnerable. It was my first opportunity to share my deepest secrets. When I was with her, I could be civil, joke, and not be judged. We were free to be ourselves and have fun."

Simone said that before she met Michael, she longed for the romance of "sharing something wonderful, loving, happy, and affirming" with the man of her dreams.

"I longed to have a feeling of unconditional trust in my special partner. He would be able to see me, 'blemishes and all,' and still be able to appreciate and affirm me. We would be as one—but without losing my own sense of identity. Those were my notions of what I wanted. Beyond that picture-book romantic thing, I didn't have a clue. I wanted just to feel free and to have romance."

Those feelings became fleeting during times of conflict in the dating stage, and the experience dampened their relationship. Often some form of bickering would follow a really enjoyable time spent together. Simone longed for more romance and less conflict.

"I really was in love with Michael, and I was young, inexperienced, and still figuring out what I wanted to be and do when I grew up. I knew that Michael wanted to get married, and I kept wondering if marriage was going to tie me up and deprive me of my personal freedom. That was my dilemma. It was a real struggle for me."

But, on Christmas Day of Simone's last year in college, Michael gave her an engagement ring at his parents' house and asked her to marry him.

"It caught me by surprise because I didn't know it was coming," she said. "I didn't know what to say. I wanted to get married, but when and how, I didn't know."

The very next day, Simone's older brother died of a drug overdose.

"I went from a state of joy and happiness to one of utter pain and despair. I desperately needed someone to help me get through it, and Michael was there. He was my support, my backbone. He helped me pull myself together."

With Michael's support, Simone completed her winter semester and graduated in the spring.

"Then we had the issue of me getting a job," she recalled. "My best offer was in Chicago. Michael said to me, 'Well, if you move to Chicago, I can't guarantee I'll be here.' I was shocked, taken aback, and didn't know what to do. I didn't want to lose Michael. So I did a dumb thing. I asked my mom for advice. This was a woman whose marriage with my father was miserable. She said, 'Well, Michael is a really great guy, and he really loves you. Do you love him?' And I said, 'Yeah, I love him.' She said, 'Well, if you love him, maybe you just should go ahead and marry him.' So that's what I did."

Simone and Michael married that September, planning their wedding over the phone, since Simone was traveling for work. She remembered the most important part being when they wrote their vows together.

"We had several talks about how we would unite but still maintain our own individuality. I just wanted the marriage to be something that would be freeing instead of constraining. And so those were the kinds of things that were in the vows. That was a good thing."

From Romance to Frustration

During the second year of their marriage, Simone became pregnant. She thought to herself, "Oh, Lord! This can't be happening. I'm just figuring out how to feel free with Michael. Children are going to really complicate things." Michael, by contrast, felt very proud.

Two years later, while still learning to be parents, their second baby was born and they moved out of the home they had rented from Michael's parents and bought their own house. Simone was ready to take the step toward home ownership but Michael wasn't. To him it seemed easier and less expensive to just stay where they were, even though it was too small for their growing family.

By that time Simone was working in Chicago during the week and flying home to Detroit on weekends. It was a rough time for Michael.

Digging beneath the Surface Frustrations for a More Meaningful Connection

Simone and Michael's more recent marital frustrations centered on a particular aspect of communication—or lack thereof—namely Simone's inability to reach Michael because he didn't answer his pager.

Describing the Surface of the Conflict

Simone described what happened.

"I can think of two incidents. The first was when I had free tickets to see Tina Turner. The second happened a week later. I had something very important to talk to him about, and he didn't return my call. I need a way to connect with Michael when important things come up during the day and I want to discuss them with him. I should not have to wait five and a half hours to get a response!"

We asked her to summarize her frustration in one sentence, but it was a challenge for her.

"I find it nearly impossible to put all of what I am experiencing in a few words." We decided to give her the homework assignment of consolidating her thoughts, and we agreed to meet again in two weeks.

But one week later she called, and had already written two full pages. She asked Melva for a little support to help her tailor it into a single page. After their conversation, Simone said that she could probably boil it down to one sentence before meeting with us the following week.

Simone showed up for the appointment with a big smile on her face. "I did it! I got this frustration down to one sentence!" She turned to Michael and said, "Michael, my bottom-line frustration is that you fail to respond to my pages. I get upset and try to talk to you about it. When I do, your temper flares up, you get angry, and you stop listening."

Jesse explained to her that this was the beginning of the mining for gold process, and encouraged her to explain her feeling more specifically.

"I feel furious when he does that!"

Melva asked if she felt anything else, and again she was stuck with too many feelings to report them in one sentence. So we gave her more homework, and a week later she returned with her reaction to Michael's behavior summed-up in three basic feelings-related words: *furious, frustrated,* and *angry.*

We helped her coax those feeling words into sentences to describe her internal process. She came up with this paragraph:

"I feel furious when I can't get hold of Michael when I need to. If there were an emergency, I could not count on Michael to respond right away. I need him to be there for me. I feel very frustrated and angry because we are not connecting. I feel let down. What's even worse is that he's not getting how important this is to me. I just feel so discounted."

"What do you do when you feel this way?" Jesse asked.

"First, I get real busy. What I realize now is that I find things to do that distract me from the frustrations I am feeling with Michael. Since I have an office in my home, I can work at my job site and also when I get home. But that does not last long. I just work until he gets home, and then I let him have it."

Dig for the Underlying Feelings

Simone had just accomplished the first big step in the gold mining process. We now helped her to identify the feelings underneath her fury and frustration.

We knew she was hurting when she reacted to Michael, so we asked her what other feelings she had. She looked at us again, almost startled.

"Other feelings? Besides furious?"

"Yes," Jesse told her. "I can see what looks like hurt in your eyes."

Melva added, "I can hear it in your voice."

"Oh, really?" Simone snapped back. "I just know *furious*."

"Upset and furious are possibly the feelings you are more familiar with," Jesse said.

"I agree," Melva told her, "I sense there are more feelings."

Simone, looking puzzled now, put her head down and tapped her right forefinger gently against her temple. Her face changed and her voice softened. She said, "What hurts me about this is that I feel ignored."

"Are there more feelings?" we asked gently. Simone was quietly crying. Her head was bent. Her hands covered her eyes.

"Yes," she said slowly. "I was just thinking about one other feeling. It's like feeling insignificant. Michael treats me like my needs are unimportant." She paused, tears streaming down her face, and then turned to Michael. "I really try to meet your needs, but when I have a need it becomes a problem."

Michael looked up and said, "Honey, I didn't know you felt this way." He put his arms around her. She buried her head in his shoulder, sobbing. After a few moments Simone composed herself, then looked at Michael and said, "It's like I'm not suppose to need."

The Fear beneath the Hurt

"What would happen if you allowed yourself to need anything from anyone?" Jesse asked. "What scares you about that?"

As Michael held her, Simone shared her fear, without prompting. She looked at him and said, "It's not being able to count on you when I really need you. What you don't understand is that is when I get really depressed. When I feel depressed, I can feel my self-esteem dropping because it feels like you don't love me, Michael, and I'm not important you."

Then, in anger, she added, "I don't want you just to be there for me when I get to the point that I'm so sad that I'm really feeling down-and-out. I want to be strong and still get the nurturing I need from you."

Michael began to cry. He started to respond to Simone, but Jesse interrupted him and advised that he just hold Simone and listen to her, for the time being.

What are your memories of similar hurts and fears?

Then Melva said, "Simone, you felt this hurt and fear before you met Michael. Tell him about that."

Simone sobbed again, as her memories came to the forefront. "I know these feelings all too well, not only in my marriage, but in my life. It was this whole thing about not feeling like much of a priority to someone I care about. I've felt like this all the way back to growing up with my parents. With my father, I felt pretty much ignored. I only felt important to him when I was taking care of my siblings and our home. Otherwise, I felt invisible. It seemed that no one cared for me or even wanted to take care of me."

Simone continued, "Make no mistake about it, my father was a good man. He worked very hard as a chauffeur and managed his real estate. Even though he stayed out all night gambling and drinking, he made sure our family was always financially secure and that each of his three children went to private schools.

"On those rare occasions when he was at home and not traveling, he was absorbed in his work. He was home physically, but not emotionally.

"I clung to those precious good times we had together when he was home and gave me his attention. I have such great memories of laughter and playing. One day I did a somersault and hit my head on the radiator. Daddy swept me up in his arms and took me to the hospital. He stayed during the surgery, and I remember the way he looked at me. I could tell that he loved me and cared about me. That was intimacy for me with Daddy. But, like with Michael, something had to be wrong before I got that."

We prompted Simone to tell us about her relationship with her mother as well, and she reported very brief good times of feeling connected.

"Those were the times when we were doing things together like baking cakes. It was great because we would laugh and talk and I would feel very close to her. I felt so loved and cared about. It felt wonderful.

"But most of the time, I felt invisible with her because she was so distracted. It is painful just thinking about it now. I wanted to have a conversation with her about what I needed. Before I could finish what I was saying, she would get depressed and begin to cry. Then she would change the subject and begin to tell me about her own problems. Not only did she cut me off from talking about what I needed; I had to console her! I had to be her confidante. She didn't hear anything I was saying about me, and what I needed. I remember this as far back as five years old."

Simone said her mother talked a lot about her dad being in a relationship with a woman called 'Momma Joanie.'

"When she wasn't talking about that, she would tell me about the man she should have married, the man she truly loved and who also loved her. I knew my mom needed a lot of support, but I was just a kid and didn't know how to give it. We never really got to what we needed from her. Whatever I needed beyond having my hair combed just wasn't there." Simone looked down at her fingers, sighed, and stared blankly at her bracelet. "By the time I was 10, my parents were living in two completely different worlds and I was feeling a real distance from both of them."

It got worse when they began a "cold war." Her father, she said, was "an absolute controller," and eventually he forced her mother to move out of their home.

"That was so hard for me." Simone's bottom lip was trembling. She began to twist a curl on the side of her temple. She looked across the room before continuing.

"With my mother gone, my father put me in charge. I was expected to manage the house and take care of my sister and older brother who was starting to experiment with drugs. I really felt set-up by my father. He told me and everyone else how competent I was. 'Look at how well she can cook, run a house, and raise everybody,' he would say with pride. 'It's a wonderful thing.' Even though I enjoyed his compliments, I felt confused. He could be so warm and loving—and then so distant.

He'd tell us all about right and wrong. And then he'd go have affairs. What made it more confusing was that when I started dating, my father was against it. It was like, *don't even look like you would be interested in being sexual. Just be the little mother and run the house.*

"Whew!" she said in exasperation.

Find the Golden Nugget: Identify Your Wants and Desires

After a short pause, Jesse asked Simone to make the connection between her frustration with Michael for not being responsive when she paged him and her feelings of not getting the nurturing and support she wanted and needed from her parents.

She responded immediately. "I absolutely know the connection. Whenever Michael does not respond to me, I have the same feelings of abandonment I did when I was a child." She looked at Michael, who was holding her again, sat straight up in her chair, cleared her throat, and said, "Michael, I need so very much for you to respond to my pages. When I have to wait, I feel alone and neglected. I feel like you don't care about me."

"But I do!" Michael interjected.

"Let her finish," Jesse advised.

Simone stopped crying, wiped her eyes, and straightened her blouse. There was silence for a few moments.

"Okay, Simone, it's time to take the next step," Jesse said. "It's time to let Michael know what you want. Think of something as extreme as you can imagine." We reminded her of the kid-in-a-candy-store metaphor and told her to think about having anything she wanted. She thought for several minutes.

"Anything I want, heh?"

"Anything you want," Jesse said.

Simone burst out laughing. "Here we go, Michael! Are you ready?"

Michael paused, squinted, and then asked, "Would Melva and Jesse have to help me to deal with this?"

Laughing even harder, Simone said, "I hope so!" She kissed him on the cheek and said, "Michael, my global desire is for you to always answer my page no more than ten seconds after I send it, 24 hours a day, seven days a week. And never, ever, get upset and raise your voice at me."

Michael replied, "Whew! I'm glad that this was the candy store experience." They bantered for a few moments and then we asked Simone to share a more realistic desire. But Simone wasn't ready to shift.

"I like this first part better."

After some coaxing she said, "Okay, okay. What might be more realistic? Let me see. Okay, Michael, I need for you to be there for me when I need you the most rather than get upset with me when I bring this up." She was looking at him. "Do you know what I mean?"

Michael nodded, "I think so."

"Even when I am upset with you, I want you to hold, nurture, and support me. I want you to say, 'Hey, we're going to work through this.' This way I won't feel like you might leave or abandon me."

Simone had identified her Gold Nugget—the things she wanted but didn't get from her parents and now wanted from Michael.

Ask For What You Want: More Realistic Desires

It was time to identify specific behaviors to fulfill that desire. We prepared Simone to shift gears and become more specific about what Michael could do. She turned to Michael and said, "I don't want you to tell me I am criticizing you or for you to get furious with me and lose your temper. I want you to understand that I need to feel cared for and recognized as a priority."

Michael interrupted. "Simone, I do care for you, even when I am upset with you. That's the part I can't seem to get across."

"But, Michael, I don't feel it! That's what I am trying to get across."

They talked for a few minutes. Then we asked Simone to be more specific.

Simone struggled with it. "I can't figure all of this out today. I need more time."

"Sounds like a good idea," Melva replied. "Give yourself at least a week. Brainstorm all of the behaviors that would show you that Michael is there for you when you need him the most and would communicate to you that he treats it as a priority. Make sure that your behavioral statements are positive, specific, in the present tense, and doable."

"This may be easier said then done," Simone replied. "I may need some help." We agreed, and also advised Michael to do the same homework so that he would be prepared when we asked him the same questions.

We got no call from Simone, but she brought a list of six behavior requests to the next session, and we asked her to select three. She pondered her list for a few minutes.

"My first request, Michael, is for the next 30 days, I want you to repeat back to me why it is important to me that you to answer my page. I want you to agree to maintain a conversational tone, stay engaged, and keep listening until you can hear me and understand how I am feeling." She looked up at Michael and cleared her throat.

"My second request is that for one week, whenever you get triggered and feel your voice rising, to just stop talking and say, 'I can't do this right now.' Then agree to try again with a calmer voice within 24 hours. That way you can let me know that you want to talk but need time to bring your anger down an octave beforehand."

She continued with her third request. "For the next three months I want you to describe whatever is triggering you, using the tools we learned in the workshop. You know, 'When you do such-and-such, I feel such-and-such'. Put your reactions into a feeling statement so that I can recognize what's going on with you."

Michael sighed, knowing that his job was to select one of Simone's requests to give her as a gift. To help him decide, we asked him to rank each request as easy, hard, or extra hard.

"Number one is to tell you what I understand about why you need me to answer your pages faster. That would be very hard if I was angry. That would be almost impossible. I'd say that number one would be extra hard. Number two is for one week to stop talking when I get angry and to set up another time to discuss my frustration in a calmer, conversational voice. That would be hard but not too hard. And number three, for the next three months to share with you how I'm feeling when I get triggered, would be hard but not impossible."

"Which one would you give me as a gift?" Simone inquired, facing Michael and putting a hand on his knee.

"Let me see... I think number three—it's hard, but doable. I would use the format Jesse and Melva taught us to describe my frustrating behavior and the feelings that got triggered within me."

Identifying the Positive Payoffs for Each Partner

Simone and Michael were doing a great job, so we took a few moments to acknowledge them for the work they had done so far. Then we led them to the next important step.

Jesse said to Simone, "Tell Michael what healing will occur for you when he gives you this gift."

Simone first thanked Michael, and then said, "I know that receiving this gift will help me to feel heard. It will also help me feel connected and important to you, Michael. I will begin to heal my past feelings of being neglected. I knew about this part before we worked with Melva and Jesse, but it makes more sense to me now. And you know what else? Hey, I think I am on a roll now! As I am thinking about this now, I already feel uplifted. That is the other healing feeling: upliftment. It's a special kind of feeling, like my Cinderella dream—being loved by my Prince Charming. Right now as I think about it I feel warm all over, and reassured."

Melva asked Michael how Simone's need to feel heard, connected, important, warm, reassured, and loved made sense to him in terms of healing.

Michael replied, "All the work we've done helps me understand that my not answering the pager was just on the surface. It makes sense to me that when I respond to Simone it demonstrates that she is important enough to be cared for and nurtured by me."

Jesse then said to Michael, "I believe that you have some very important information to share with Simone. Namely, what would develop within you when you give her that gift?"

"Yeah, I've been thinking about this. I'm ready. I know what I want to say." He turned to Simone and reached for her hand. "Granting you this gift will help me get more in touch with my feelings beneath the anger, like I did during our counseling and our group meetings. I will develop my ability to articulate these feelings in such a way that you will understand me—and I know that will demonstrate how much I love you."

Michael continued, "The other ability I will develop is the ability to understand and value your needs by seeing your frustrations from your perspective. What will be difficult for me in giving you this gift will be to follow through by reshaping my own priorities, but I'll work on that."

"Michael, I am so impressed. I didn't know you gave this so much thought," Simone said with teary eyes.

Before continuing, Melva gave them time to savor their special moment of loving connection. Then she emphasized that following through on these requests might not be as easy as it seemed, and reminded them that it required a real commitment from both of them. Melva told Simone that at first it would probably be enjoyable to receive her gift from Michael. But she cautioned her that after a while, the old fears of neglect and abandonment could surface again as Michael tried hard to be consistent with his new behavior but occasionally slipped.

"You may find Simone reacting in the same old ways each time you don't follow through," Melva explained to Michael. "So don't 'flip out' if you see Simone reacting in the old familiar ways. Just be aware that she has been triggered again by your old patterns of relating. Remind yourself that she is likely feeling neglected and abandoned once again. I encourage you to respond appropriately to the feelings of hers that lie below the surface. At those moments, Simone probably needs to be heard, feel connected, and realize that she is important to you. Reach out to her and re-establish the connection."

Jesse turned to Simone. "Simone, your challenge may be in receiving Michael's gift. Even though it was painful and uncomfortable, your old ways of relating created a familiar, emotional distance. You must now stretch beyond the familiar to embrace the closeness, connection, and deepening intimacy that your new way of relating will offer you."

If they felt themselves slipping back to the old familiar patterns, Melva urged them, they needed to shift gears, get back on track, and remind themselves of the gifts they were sharing, and remain steadfastly committed to the process.

Two Different Realities
Michael's Reality

It was time to hear Michael's side of the story—his reality. Jesse turned to him and said, "Each of you have your own perspective on the situation and it is essential that both of your realities be heard, understood, and acknowledged by the other. We may learn how your early childhood experiences influence your current reactions, as we have done with Simone."

Describe the Surface of the Conflict

Michael began. "Man, I gotta tell you, I did get triggered when Simone got upset about those two pager incidents."

He admitted that Simone had described the second incident accurately. "I was in the gym when she paged. I didn't get the message because I didn't have the pager on me; it was in the locker room." He sighed, then continued. "So we had another blow-up. The frustration for me was that I was being asked to perform at a level that was unreasonable."

His voice rose an octave "So I forgot my pager," he snapped. "It doesn't happen often. It's just one of those things that happens in the normal course of a day. I was angry. I was beyond pissed. So I rebuffed her.

"And then after we talked about it, Simone said she wasn't sure I got it. I did get it. I really did get it. I just felt criticized, like, *Where were you, what were you doing that you didn't get my page, you couldn't return my call?* I felt like that was what she felt underneath. Like I wasn't trusted."

Michael said that for him, this was another example of her wanting him to do things her way. "She generously provides unsolicited instruction on how to do it, and I want her to stop. She often tells me what to do, and when I agree to do it, she checks behind me. She actually asks me several times if I did it or not. Of course, her instructions are to do it her way, even when I am feeling pretty confident about getting it done my way. Answering my pager when I can isn't about neglecting or abandoning Simone; it's about me being realistic about what I can do!"

Melva said to Michael, "I can hear the frustration in your voice. Do you have any other feelings right now?"

Michael replied, "I probably do. I think I have more difficulty than Simone does figuring out my feelings because I don't generally describe my experiences in this way. Maybe furious is the other feeling."

Michael said he felt angry, furious, and controlled. "That is why I get defensive. I don't like being questioned or monitored. I completely block her out when things get difficult between us. I fall into coping the way that has worked for me all of my life, by finding some kind of outside activity to occupy my time. It does not matter what it is—going to the bar or working on a political campaign, playing softball or tag football. As a boy, I could always find a reason not to be home. That's what my father did, he was never home. He'd leave early in the morning and get back at about eleven at night. That was his way of dealing with problems. But it actually created huge problems for him, and it's created huge problems for me."

Michael became more aware of his anger. "When distracting myself doesn't work, I become furious and yell at her."

"You sure do," Simone inserted. "And it gets real stressful for me when you get to that point."

Jesse interrupted them to keep Michael focused on going below the surface of their conflict.

Digging for the Underlying Feelings

Melva said, "The reason you get stuck here is because you focus on your anger about each other's frustrating behaviors. I know there is some hurt and fear underneath the frustration and anger, and I am curious about those underlying feelings."

What's the hurt below the surface feeling?

Michael said, "The criticism is what hurts the most. Initially I feel criticized because,"— he turned to Simone, who was looking at him intently— "I really do take your needs seriously. I really feel like I am working to be attentive, accessible, and responsive. What hurts the most is when you don't acknowledge that. I feel like I am being asked to perform at a level that is unreasonable with no room for error."

Simone had not realized until then that she gave more negative than positive feedback. "I had no idea that I wasn't giving very much positive feedback. I'm sorry." What he had explained was new information to her.

What's the fear below the hurt?

"There is more," he said. "Remember when you figured out what was scary for you underneath your frustration?"

"Yes, honey, I remember."

"Well I figured out what is scary for me. What scares me about all of this is that I might get to the point of you perceiving me as being inadequate, in addition to feeling controlled. That's what happens when I feel like I am getting a lot of direction from you with very little positive feedback."

What are your memories of similar hurts and fears?

Michael had identified his feelings beneath the surface of his frustration and anger. The time was right to make a connection to his relationship history.

We asked him when he had felt these feelings before. Michael dropped his head, took a deep breath, and said, "This reminds me of all the times in my life of not feeling I did anything well enough for my parents. They just didn't make me feel that I was competent at being able to do anything and that made me feel awful."

Michael's parents were performance oriented, he said, working hard, motivating their children to work hard, and prescribing lots of rules and expectations.

"There weren't any warm, 'touchy' things going on between us as far back as I can remember. My parents' relationship was pretty much a cold war—lots of arguments, no hugging and kissing, that kind of stuff. It was very, very controlled. The family rule was, 'Never let the public know that you don't get along.'"

Michael's father was a staff sergeant in the Marines and a military policeman. "Everything with my father was *yes sir, no sir*. We did what he said, when he said it, the way he said it, and that's the way it was. Mistakes and violations brought physical punishment. We never had a father-son talk, never had any two-way conversations, never hugged. Even to this day, he has never said to my brother or me, *I love you, I'm proud of you, son*, none of that. What was important to my parents was to make sure that we were strong enough to survive."

He was putting his finger on early childhood wounds that had an impact on how he was relating to Simone.

"The times I recall being closest to my father were all performance related. I started Little League when I was about eight or nine. In the beginning I wasn't very good so I rode the bench a lot. But for my dad, that was, like, no way. So every Saturday morning, just like the army, I would get up at 6:00 a.m. to go practice with my dad. I became a very good baseball player, but it was a real challenge."

Michael recalled that his mother's father, who lived with their family for a short while before he died, was the one who provided his only memory of feeling some warmth and connection. "He could relate to what I was experiencing without necessarily finding a reason to criticize or punish me for it."

Michael's mom was a hardworking woman who was committed to fighting poverty in the community. "She eventually had a job where she was out of town four days a week. Her mission for my brother and me was no drugs, no jail, go to school and get good grades, and go to college. She figured that the best way to protect us was to keep us in church and involved in athletics. There was always someplace to go or someplace to be and chores to do. Like my dad, she was very performance oriented. None of that kissing and hugging, *I love you, son,* kind of stuff."

Michael said that he learned early in life how to avoid close, intimate relationships. "I just knew how to survive, how to be alone, how to take care of my own issues, how to suppress my feelings, how to get on with it or get over it. That's what I was taught: *If you fall down and scrape your knee, get up! What are you lying there for? What are you crying for?* My parents would give me a whipping and then tell me, *Don't cry.*

The more you would cry, the more they would beat you. You just had to learn how to get over it. We didn't talk about hurt or fear. That was a sign of weakness. I was taught that I ought to work, make a living, or produce something for the world to make it better. I followed the family script—to do something productive."

Melva asked Michael to make a connection between his memories of relating to his parents and what he was experiencing with Simone.

"The pager incidents triggered me in two ways. First I think you are being unreasonable when you expect me to always answer my pager right away. This reminds me of growing up and living in a household where my parents were very controlling. Second, I feel criticized because these were exceptions, not the rule. That, too, feels familiar. Everything had to be perfect, exactly the way my parents wanted it, how they wanted it, when they wanted it. Doing it my way was unacceptable. I didn't get the benefit of the doubt from my parents back then, and I don't get it now from you, Simone. Every little thing becomes magnified into a big thing. I'm not perfect, I'm sorry. I didn't have any ill intention, I just felt like you didn't give me a fair shake."

Jesse asked Michael to tell us what he wanted most from his parents that he didn't get. His eyes became watery as he held back tears. In spite of his best effort to stay in control, tears ran down his cheeks. He quickly brushed them away and said, "All I ever wanted was to be listened to and understood by my mother and to be accepted and loved by my father."

Michael had made a connection between his past and present. He was ready to identify the golden nugget.

Finding the Gold Nugget of Wants and Desires

Michael had done his homework and knew what came next. "It is time for me to tell Simone what my global desire is, right?"

"Right!" Jesse confirmed. "A desire so outrageous that it would be impossible for Simone to fulfill."

Michael, with a smile and a laugh, said to Simone, "Get ready!"

"I started getting ready when we got to this part."

"It's not that bad!" Michael reassured with a smile. "When you page me, I want you to wait for me to answer without getting upset."

He laughed and Melva asked why. He said it was because he saw how absurd his request was and knew there was no way Simone could fulfill it.

"You got that right!" Simone chimed in.

Michael continued, "I want you to view me as being a competent husband who loves and cares about you in everything he does. I really want your 100 percent trust in me, in everything I might take on now and in the future. I hope you can hear this, Simone."

"I do," she said.

Michael was then aware of his unconscious, unrealistic expectations of Simone. He had demanded that she not "get upset" when he failed to respond to her pages. Once he was aware of the absurdity of his expectation, he could make a more realistic request.

Forging the Golden Keys: Michael Asks for What He Wants

Jesse asked Michael to think of three specific, doable requests that he could ask of Simone.

Michael turned to Simone. "My first request is that for the next three months, I want you to listen and understand my explanation when I cannot answer my pager right away. My second request is, for the next three months, I need you to be clear about what you expect from me, and I want to hear you say to me that you know I can do it. I want you to trust me to do it my way without interference and to ask for a meeting if the outcomes are not achieved. Give me the chance to make the mistake. If I don't do it right, I can correct it."

Michael continued, "My third request is, if you approach me about a strategy that you feel very strongly is the correct or most needed one, then you take the assignment and do it. If your approach is really important to you, then that's maybe something you should take on yourself instead of asking me to do it the way you want me to do it.

"And, my fourth request is…"

Simone interrupted Michael. "Your fourth request? You only get three! Right, Jesse and Melva?"

Melva responded "Right! If you choose, Simone, you can listen to all four and then decide if you want to consider three or four. You still get to choose."

Simone said, "Oh, maybe I like this better, to have more choices. Okay, I want to hear the fourth one."

"All right," Michael said. "My fourth request is for the next thirty days you tell me that you trust me to do whatever I agree to do and that you have a preferred way of doing it, which is thus and so. But I choose what's best for me and you accept whatever way I decide."

Now that Michael had made four requests, Melva asked Simone to indicate which ones would be easy, hard, or extra hard.

Simone summarized the first one: "Listening to your explanation without letting you know how upset I am in the moment is hard, maybe extra hard. The second one about agreeing or stating the outcome I would like—this is hard, but not real hard. But it might be a challenge if we get hung up on making a mutually satisfactory agreement. Number three is to just do it myself and not involve you if it's important to me how it gets done. That one wouldn't work if it were something I need your assistance to do, so it is another extra-hard one. Number four is to tell you that there's something I would like for you to do. If I have a preference on how it is to be accomplished, to say so but to allow you to decide how to do it. This is not easy either because I'm still learning to trust you completely about things that might be very important to me. So as a gift, I would like to choose number three. For the next thirty days, I will give you the gift of sharing my preference, if I have one, but trusting you to do it your way."

Michael sported a wide grin when he heard the gift from Simone.

Identifying the Positive Payoffs for Each Partner

"Okay, Michael," Jesse said, "our idea is that healing will occur for you. Would you complete this sentence? Thank you, Simone, your granting me this gift will enable me to _____."

Michael looked down at his homework notes. "Thank you, Simone. Receiving your gift will help me to begin to heal the wounds of feeling controlled, inadequate, and not trusted to handle responsibilities, both in our relationship and from my childhood. I'll feel confident in your belief in me and at peace with my own feelings of confidence. I will begin to feel unconditionally loved."

Michael then got up, walked to the window, and looked out without saying a word. Jesse asked, "What's happening, Michael?" but got no response at first. After a long pause, while still looking out the window, he said, "I really would feel it."

Simone got up and joined him. In a near whisper she asked, "Are you ready to hear what would happen for me?"

Michael did not answer right away. He kept looking out the window. Simone waited. "Let me know when you are ready."

Michael slowly turned around. His eyes were red, and his head was down. Almost inaudibly he said, "I'm ready."

"Okay," Simone said quietly. "You're welcome. Granting you this gift will help me to overcome my inability to trust. I'll know that what's important to me is important to you. It will also help me to feel unburdened—to just let things be. I will know that I've got a partner who will help share my burdens. I know control is an issue for you, so this will also help me overcome my need to control outcomes. It will help me to grow to trust our agreements and ultimately help me feel reassured."

Jesse reminded Michael and Simone that doing this work would not be easy. It would take a conscientious, ongoing commitment, backed up with a clear intention. "However, you have both described a tremendous payoff of healing and growth that would lead to a feeling of a deeper connection with one another."

Identifying Your "Golden Nugget"— Knowing What You Want

Michael and Simone demonstrated that beneath the surface of frustration is an unfulfilled desire. Specific feelings of aloneness, neglect, being unloved, and not cared about surfaced for Simone when Michael did not respond to her. Now that she had dug beneath the surface, she was able to describe having the same feelings of abandonment as a child.

It was important for Simone to describe her desire in global terms, to honor her deepest desires. And while she wanted Michael to answer every page from her within ten seconds, 24 hours per day and seven days a week, she knew that was unrealistic. The same was true for her second request, for him to *never, ever* get upset or raise his voice at her. Simone was, however, able to get more specific and formulate more realistic desires for Michael to be there for her by responding promptly to her pages and to control his reactive, angry impulses when she wanted to discuss important topics.

Simone's healing will be very significant. She will feel more secure knowing that they are going to work calmly through their challenges together to resolve their issues. Simone will be able to begin healing feelings of abandonment experienced both in the "here and now" and from her children.

Michael's parents consistently modeled the ways that he learned to express his upset. His new response helped him to contain his typical reactive behavior of being upset and angry with Simone. By containing his impulses, he and Simone will be able to work through their issues so that she will get what she needs and be able to have 100% trust in him.

Initially, most couples enjoy both giving and receiving the new behaviors that they have agreed to give each other as gifts. That changes quickly, however, if one of the partners fails to continue to follow through consistently. Memories of previous hurts and fears usually re-surface again, often with greater intensity. If this happens, it is imperative that the couple discuss the situation, take whatever corrective action is required, and recommit to following through on their new behavior requests.

We can not overemphasize the importance of partners following through consistently in honoring their behavior requests to each other. It is an essential path to a deeper feeling of commitment, trust, love, and connection.

Update on Simone and Michael

Michael and Simone were not always sure if their marriage would survive. At times it seemed that the fairly tale was becoming more of a nightmare. They knew they loved each other, but often they could not stand living together. When they became frustrated, they would have arguments and verbal fights.

Simone said, "We started early on with fights. We struggled for years. We were so stubborn, so set in our ways. It's really painful when you don't know how to deal with it."

In spite of their love for each other and their very best efforts, they, like many couples, could not find resolution. In fact, the harder they tired, the more frustrated they became.

Even when they decided to attend our weekend couples' workshop, Simone said they didn't hold out much hope.

"Things were so bad between us that we said, *What the heck, it couldn't hurt.* But honestly, we both wondered if things were beyond repair."

At the workshop, they learned how to dig beneath the surface feelings to discover the origins of their frustrations with each other. They followed up with personal coaching and reported significant repair, healing, and growth. After that time, they began finding deeper connection with each other, more laugher and fun, greater respect, more trust, and more self-confidence.

"Now," Simone told us later, "we are doing better than we ever have in our 25 years together. We are happy. We express the love that has always been there and look forward to growing old together and sharing deeper and more joyful experiences."

Michael added, "We understand each other better. We are committed to respecting and caring for each other's feelings, wants, and needs. We have decided to make them, and each other, a priority in our lives."

Simone said, "The model I learned as a child was, *We're staying together for the kids, but we're not going to talk to each other.*"

"Yes," agreed Michael, "neither of us was raised with good role models for intimacy. Our parents didn't know how to deal with the stresses and strains of marriage. They did the best they knew how but ended up doing a poor job of dealing effectively with their differences."

"We have decided that we would create a different model for our children," said Simone. "They would see us going through conflicts, dealing with frustrations constructively, and being mutually supportive and respectful."

Michael and Simone had clearly embarked on a new phase of their journey. To sustain them they would need commitment, patience, and perseverance. It isn't easy and it involves continuous hard work!

They would become triggered at times by each other's behaviors and likely become reactive—following old patterns of behavior. The discomfort they would feel could become a new trigger—one that would help them to start the Mining for Gold process. The more they discovered about themselves and the personal vulnerabilities that triggered reactive behaviors, the less blaming and criticism they would have for each other. And the more fulfilling their relationship would become.

The "Fairly Tale" Ends In Divorce

In spite of their valiant attempts to overcome their differences and reconcile, Michael and Simone's marriage eventually led to divorce. A few years afterward, both were continuing to adjust to their new lives as single, divorced people. One aspect of vital importance to them was to figure out ways to co-parent their one teenage daughter and two adult sons. They were also committed to being friends in a new context. They decided to share their perceptions of their current situations separately.

Simone after the Divorce

Simone reported that she and Michael still loved each other and she believed that it would always be that way. She explained that as much as she loved

Michael and he loved her, he wasn't able to stretch and grow to meet her needs or follow through on the behaviors he agreed to change.

She said they struggled with the issue of fidelity throughout their almost 28 years of marriage. Simone decided that she could no longer struggle with that. "If he wasn't able to resolve this at age 50, it was unlikely that he ever would." Although she loved him, she no longer wanted to be married to him. It was too painful to be hurt over and over again with his broken promises of change.

She felt disappointment and anger, but mostly disappointment and sadness, she said, that they couldn't get it right despite all their love for one another. The lesson for her was that you may be "in love" and not be right for each other. "We really wanted to be together but there were core things we couldn't resolve –things that were about who we are."

She wanted Michael to be happy deep within himself and wanted the same for herself. She decided they couldn't do it together. The healing for them would have to occur as separate individuals.

With tears in her eyes, Simone said that she decided what she wanted, needed, and desired in a husband; and that she was not going to compromise or accept anything less. She was also clear that it was not about either of them being "good" or "bad" people. It was about what it takes to develop, maintain, and sustain a mutually satisfying, long term, committed relationship over time. Some people are better able to do that than others, based upon both the conscious and unconscious decisions they have made because of their experiences with significant people in their lifetime.

Simone went back to school to pursue a new career in education, excited about life and all of the unexpected opportunities to come. In spite of the pain and disappointments she had with Michael, she recalled the good times with him. She said she was grateful for the beautiful, special moments she shared with Michael, and she wanted to be a blessing to the world and to be open to her own blessings from the world.

Michael after the Divorce

"I'm still trying to deal with the divorce and losing my job." Michael explained. "I'm adjusting fairly well. I still miss Simone. I miss the good parts of the relationship—being home with her and the children. I feel a significant void.

"Two years prior to the divorce was actually the beginning of the end. A lot happened during those two years. When I lost my job and couldn't find employment, I felt that my role as the anchor and security blanket for my family had dissolved. Our savings eroded away and in spite of my best efforts, I could not find a way to replenish it. I was going deeper into a depression and my choices about how to feel better were mistakes. I was ashamed of myself and afraid of hurting Simone. I didn't want to lose her. Right now, I can't say I'm happy, but little by little I'm coping better, and at times I am at peace. I've come to grips with how I contributed to the divorce. I own my weaknesses and am seeking help because I'm still trying to figure it all out and get the answers I need. In the past, I've not always been willing to look at myself and admit my mistakes—probably because of guilt. I have regrets and now I can speak about them without debilitating shame that throws me into a tailspin. As much as I loved Simone, there were still some things missing in our relationship. We tried but failed."

Melva asked him to elaborate.

"We tried the tools you taught us and had some success. But I continued to have a longing—a need for a special kind of connection—and it just wouldn't go away. I tried to communicate it to Simone and maybe I just didn't do a good enough job because we just couldn't seem to get to that place deep within me where I wanted and needed to connect. This journey is teaching me a lot about myself. Probably the most significant growth for me has been about infidelity."

Jesse asked what he had learned.

"I have learned that trying to fill that yearning for connection by the temporary 'fix' of an affair does not solve the problems in your marriage. No matter how difficult, distasteful, or painful it might be, you must be willing to communicate about any and every thing in your marriage. No subject should be excluded. There were times when I needed to talk to Simone about my feeling the need to see another woman. Talking to her about it probably sounds crazy. There was something I wasn't getting in our marriage that I felt the need to get elsewhere. Talking about it would have given us a chance to deal with it. There could have been something of value for both of us if we could have had those kinds of discussions. However, we didn't. Simone would probably have become angry and I can understand why. But I also believe such discussions would have produced a better outcome because we would have used the tools you taught us to work through all that. We would have talked it out and then I probably would not have followed through with some of the poor decisions I made."

Despite how much he was hurting, he still believed Simone loved him. "We are both trying to sort our way through this without walking away angry. We are trying to heal and remain friends."

Michael had a current girlfriend. He emphasized "just one" and laughed.

"I am trying to express my feelings, wants, and needs and be honest with her no matter what the cost. I'm telling her the truth about where I am at any given moment. Based on my honesty, she can decide if she wants to continue in the relationship or not." He told her he was not ready to consider marriage because he was not over Simone.

Michael was becoming increasingly comfortable being alone with himself. While married, he was the center of his family as "provider" and "protector." Afterwards, he played a more peripheral role.

"When I was working," Michael said, "my time was structured around my job. My boss made my decisions about how I would spend my time. Now that I no longer have that high-stress, demanding, structured, 24 hour 7 days a week job, I have had to learn how to structure my own time. This is new for me and I'm learning how to do this and enjoy the freedom.

"I have also needed to put some emotional distance between me and my parents and siblings. I have needed time to think, figure things out and feel my feelings and let it be okay. I have needed time to be alone to feel my hurt and pain without trying to numb it with booze or women. Releasing my feelings has helped me get through the rough days. I still have my melancholy moments. Rather than lasting a week or several days, now they last a few moments. I still awaken each day missing Simone. I've been journaling, meditating, praying and owning my deepest fears. I now realize that I don't have to be in control every waking moment. I can be free to feel my emotions and allow them to wash through me."

He said he was enjoying learning how to be an independent businessperson. "I am networking, meeting people, and paying attention to those I meet. I allow myself to learn from each person I encounter." With tears in his eyes he said, "What has surprised me the most is how much we are all alike. We all have hopes and dreams for ourselves and our families. And even when we falter, we keep getting up and trying again. Within us is this compelling need to fulfill our aspirations and dreams. I am determined to achieve mine and I am committed to helping those I love and care about to achieve theirs."

CHAPTER 6
DEBORAH ANN AND CHRIS'S STORY
BALANCING ROMANCE AND WORK

"You Don't Spend Enough Time with Me"

Chris and Deborah Ann taught us that the trauma of childhood does not go away despite our best attempts to ignore it. Instead, it continually emerges to rear its ugly head within current relationships. Unfinished business from our past leaks into our present, and is the trigger for many of our ongoing, unresolved relationship frustrations and conflicts. The good news is that within the context of a committed love relationship, we can begin to heal the past and experience greater joy in the present.

For Deborah Ann and Chris, their pasts kept creeping into their present day-to-day relationship. However, with commitment and dedication, they finally found a way to keep themselves on track with the love and the kind of caring connection they had always wanted. The journey took time and was painful, but the payoff was worth all the patience and effort. The smiles we saw on their faces and the way they looked affectionately at each other as they shared their story are powerful testimony to what they have accomplished.

Deborah Ann was an attractive, petite, spunky, and lively Hispanic woman with short, curly hair. Chris described her with a sense of pride. "Her smile is one of genuine sincerity. The softness in her tone warms your heart. When she talks with or listens to you, you feel her positive, caring energy. Her laughter charms anyone into being her friend."

Chris was a white man with blue eyes that Deborah Ann said are deep like the ocean. Deborah Ann described him as handsome and loving. "He's a man's man and my very best friend and lover. Over the years, the quality I have loved about Chris most is his willingness to change himself in a way that contributes to a better marriage. I love his devotion to our children and me, and his ability to forgive and forget. He has been present to share the good as well as the bad times together. Twenty years later, after all the many ups and downs, I am still glad I said, *I do.*"

Deborah Ann and Chris were both in their 40s. They met in their 20s, had been married 21 years, and had two children, a boy and a girl.

Chris was a corporate executive in an extremely demanding position. Deborah Ann was a stay-at-home mom, a homemaker, and a student.

Their Attraction

Deborah Ann spoke first. "We met in our 20s. I had just ended a very painful and abusive relationship and I was feeling very hurt and alone. When I met Chris, I needed somebody to talk to. And, oh, did we talk. He would come over my apartment, and we would talk until two or three o'clock in the morning. The more we talked, the more I was able to cope with the drama and trauma in my life. That was when the floodgates opened."

Chris said, "When I met Deborah Ann, I was ready to find the right person. I was in a lot of pain and it was hard to deal with. At the time, I only knew how to numb it with beer, bourbon, cocaine, and marijuana. Underneath was a lonely man looking for someone to share his life with.

"At that time, my idea of having a relationship with a woman was maybe having a bottle of wine, smoking a joint, watching the sunset, and listening to some rock music. So when I met Deborah Ann, it was during a period of my life when it wasn't cool to show another person that I was hurting. I thought it was manlier to be in control of things.

"I was attracted to her right away. The more we talked, the more I was attracted to her. I felt my pain of loneliness melting away. Then I started feeling this chemistry and connection that I had not experienced with anybody else. I wondered if I had found my soul mate. Little by little, we found ourselves falling into a loving relationship. Deborah Ann was someone who had lived and seen the world beyond Chicago, somebody who'd been beyond the suburbs, and that I added to the attraction I felt for her. I knew she was somebody I could bond with."

Melva asked Chris how long the romantic stage in their relationship lasted.

"About three years," he said, "while we were both working, and before our girl was born." Chris turned to Deborah Ann, smiled at her, and said, "I remember those early days. They were like magic for me."

From Romance to Frustration

Chris said the magic began to disappear when their daughter was born. "Having kids changes everything. The private time we experienced totally changed. In the midst of a wonderful, passionate moment, we would hear the pitter-patter of little feet coming down the hallway. We'd jump up and scramble for our clothes to get dressed really fast. Then we would sit up straight on opposite sides of the bed. We'd get ourselves together just before she ran into our room. Then we'd said, 'Hi, we're just sorting our socks.' After that we put a lock on our door. We handled that problem pretty well."

Deborah Ann said that things began to get bad for them when they locked horns about how to discipline their daughter. "At the time, I didn't realize that we were competitive. We had not figured out how to do this together."

Melva asked Deborah Ann to give us an example of the conflict they experienced.

"Well," she said, "When our daughter was about one year old she was running around in a restaurant, having a great time. People at other tables were watching us. Chris's patience grew thin. He grabbed her and made her sit down. I think he scared her because after that she didn't budge. I thought that was punishment enough; but Chris wanted to make sure she understood that she was behaving poorly. So he made her sit in her room when we got home. She cried and cried. I couldn't bear it. She was just one year old. She didn't understand. I really started to break up that night. I was extremely angry. The honeymoon was over."

Deborah Ann remembered that sometimes Chris was the one who wanted to give in to their daughter. "When we were trying to wean our daughter off the bottle, Chris wanted to give her a bottle right away because he couldn't stand to listen to her crying. He said it hurt too much. I said, 'No, we can't do that. The doctor said not to do that.' We argued about that. I would not give in just because he was peeved."

When they started taking parenting classes they realized that every time one of them was saying *yes* to their daughter, the other was saying *no*. They were just beginning to learn to stop the confusion when their son was born, and the power struggle over who was in charge of the parenting started up again.

Jesse asked Deborah Ann and Chris if this frustration was the one they wanted to explore in the Mining for Gold process. Deborah Ann was ready with her answer: "No, we want to deal with something that started a long time ago and has gotten worse."

Deborah Ann's irritation with Chris had set the ball of frustrations rolling, so she laid out the problem. "I really get angry when Chris isn't physically or emotionally available. It started years ago when we decided that I would become a stay-at-home mom and Chris would provide for all of us. The problem is Chris got so busy at work that he isn't emotionally available to me. I want so very much for him to set aside more time for us. I seem to be second, and sometimes third, to the people he works with. I want to feel like the most important person in his life, and I do not. He gives me time when I asked for it, but I have to asked for it, then put it on the calendar, figure out the possible suggestions, plan it, and hire the baby-sitter."

Deborah Ann described a recent incident when she felt like Chris put her last. "He was out of town on business, and I was waiting to hear from him. All day long I waited for a phone call. When he finally called, it was 11 o'clock at night. I didn't answer the phone. I knew exactly what I was doing. I just watched the phone ring. While it was ringing, I was thinking, *I'm not going to answer. I'll be damned if I'm the last thing that you're thinking of.*"

Chris called again the next morning. "I was getting ready to take our daughter to school. I just looked at the phone and let it ring. I was thinking, *I'm still not going to answer. You're going to miss me.* That's the message I wanted to convey. *You're going to miss me.*" Several hours later Deborah Ann decided to call him and leave a message on his voicemail. She said, "Thank you for calling me at 11 p.m. However, I feel very hurt that I was the last thing on your agenda."

She admitted to us "I do not know how to get beyond this."

Mining for Gold: Digging Beneath the Surface Frustrations for a More Meaningful Connection

Describe the Surface of the Conflict

Melva asked Deborah Ann to tell us more about what the conflict looked like on the surface. For instance, what happened when she brought the problem to his attention?

"At first he would tell me that he wanted to relax, or he got angry," she said. "When he said he wanted to relax, he meant he wanted to sit around talking. Talking could be fun to talk if my romantic needs were being met, but they weren't. What frustrated me the most was that when I tried get him to actually listen to me, he would just blow up with anger."

Jesse asked what she felt before the blow up.

"When Chris doesn't call, or calls me at the end of the day, first I get angry and do passive aggressive things like not answering the phone. I make him wait. When that doesn't work I stuff my anger, I bury it, and I sweep it under the rug. Then one of two things happens. Either he gets so angry at me that he blows up and I close down, or the little emotional pebble inside me becomes a gigantic mountain. If that happens I blow up, and get so angry that I sometimes insult him. But generally I just close down and clam up. Maybe that explains why I have only been intimate with a few people. Even today, I feel I'm more closed than open. It's an issue that keeps coming up, over and over again.

Digging for the Underlying Feelings

What was the Hurt Underneath Your Anger?

Deborah Ann became silent, appearing to be lost in her thoughts and feelings. Holding her head down, she began to cry. She asked Chris for a tissue. She had gotten in touch with the hurt below her anger.

Melva proceeded. "So what I am hearing is that when Chris blows up you close down and after you blow up and insult him, you close down. Is that accurate?" Deborah Ann nodded. Melva continued. "Will you describe the feeling you experience when you shut down?"

A few moments later Deborah Ann raised her head and spoke. "I feel terrified when Chris blows up because it creates a lot of distance between us and that hurts me because it is painful to feel so lonely. It hurts when I feel abandoned." She looked down again and clasped her hands tightly, trying to maintain her composure and not burst into tears again.

"I am tired of crying about this," she said.

What was the Fear Below the Hurt?

Jesse then asked Deborah Ann what scared her the most about feeling lonely and abandoned.

She turned to Chris, paused, took a deep breath, and said "Chris, what you don't understand is that although you have never hurt me in any physical way, your explosiveness terrifies me. You are so volatile that it seems like you are in some kind of trance when you get angry and I avoid you and feel lonely and abandoned. I am getting tired of feeling so hurt and scared, Chris.

How many times have I told you about these feelings and that I am afraid that I will never be as important to you as your work? How many times have I told you that I am terrified of always feeling lonely, sad, and abandoned? I really don't think you get it. You say you do, but continue to ignore me. I don't know what else to tell you or to do."

Her tone was angry. She broke eye contact with Chris.

What are Your Earliest Memories of these Hurts and Fears?

It was the perfect time to explore the connection between past and present. If we addressed the anger she had just expressed, we would remain on the surface of their issue, so we dug deeper into memories of those painful feelings.

"Deborah Ann, what do these feelings remind you of, from before you met Chris?" Jesse asked.

She made the connection immediately. "With all the therapy I have had, I am very clear about the connection. I feel like I am living at home with my angry parents who would blow their tops for any minor reason. They were so engrossed with their anger that they pretty much acted like they forgot I was around."

Melva asked Deborah Ann to tell us more about what living in her family was like. Deborah Ann began to weep. Jesse told her to take her time and let us know when she was ready to talk. After a few minutes, she continued. "I grew up in a household with parents who drank heavily and spent the majority of their time together yelling and fighting. When I was very young I saw my father physically abuse my mother over and over again. I vividly remember one time, when I was three years old. We were on a family outing at a campsite with some friends. We stayed in bungalows, and the rooms were separated like in a hospital—with sheets. The light was on, so I could see the images on the other side of the curtain. I remember my father just cold-cocking my mother. The next morning she had a huge black eye; with no explanation, and they acted as though everything was all right."

Deborah Ann said the incident terrorized her to the point that the only way she could figure out how to deal with it was to make herself invisible. "At a very young age I learned how to disappear and stay out of my father's way, to avoid making contact with his belt and shoes."

Her mother beat her as well, when she about 12, she said, and she had no one to talk to about it. "Yet my mother used me as a confidante and told me all of the woes of her relationship with my father. However, I do not recall her ever sitting down and being a confidante for me."

Melva asked Deborah Ann to tell us more about feeling lonely and abandoned as a child.

"My parents would leave in the morning and come back whenever they felt like it. My oldest brother and sister would leave whenever they wanted. There I was, stuck with taking care of the two little boys. I used to hate it because I wanted to go outside, but I had to stay home instead. I was constantly waiting for my parents to come home or waiting for them to stop what they were doing. If I needed help with something, I didn't know who to rely on or who to call. I was so scared because I had no way of knowing where they were. And when they did get home, I couldn't talk to them about it."

Without our prompting, Deborah Ann began to connect her childhood feelings with her present. "I wear a mask of being a strong, independent woman. And I am. But behind that mask is this scared little girl. There is fear when Chris goes away to work. Now I am raising two children. Sometimes that feeling comes back of being stuck, even though I know I'm an adult. I can get in the car and go someplace. But I have to fight something within myself that tells me I cannot go. I grew up hungry for an opportunity to have a relationship with someone I could talk to and share the pain that I lived with for so many years. When Chris and I first met I had that opportunity. I long to share the pain I experience in day to day living, instead of standing in the midst of the chaos that I experienced in my parents' house."

Jesse asked Deborah Ann what was it that she really wanted from her parents that she didn't get.

Deborah Ann began to cry and Chris put his arm around her. "All I ever wanted was to feel important to them—like I was a priority in their life sometimes. But I never got that."

Finding the Gold Nugget: Identify Your Wants and Desires

Melva told Deborah Ann how her past and present experience made sense and invited her to consider a new outcome. To bring her underlying desire to the surface, it was best for Deborah Ann to begin with her global desire.

"Deborah Ann," Jesse said, "we know you are very clear about what you don't want. We are now ready to support you to invite Chris to give you what you want in a different way.

"Oh!" she said. "I know what I want. I want not to feel so hurt and scared."

"That's a good start," Melva said. "Now imagine having a magic wand in your hand. When you wave it you can have whatever you want from Chris to replace your feelings of sadness, loneliness, and abandonment. If you could have anything in the world from him to heal these feelings, what would it be?" Melva urged her to ask for something outrageous, something way beyond his ability to provide.

Deborah Ann looked confused and asked for some time to think. After a 10-minute break, a little talk with Chris, and a few additional minutes alone, she returned with her answer. "I figured it out," she said with a smile on her face.

She walked up to Chris and sat on his lap. Looking him straight in the eye she said, "Chris, my global desire is I want to be first in every area of your life, no matter what. That means I want you to give all of your attention to me before you even consider giving attention to your work.

We enjoyed her good feelings with her for a few minutes before Jesse asked her the next question. "Deborah Ann, now we would like for you to let Chris know about your more realistic desire."

"I thought about that. I am clear that I want Chris to show me that I am his number one customer all the time in our relationship. I need him to be in touch with me during his day. Like check-in during the day, not at the end. And I know this will not happen all the time because Chris does have to work and take care of his employees. Because I have put so much energy into being upset and thinking about what I don't want, I need to think about his some more." She agreed to ponder it in the week ahead.

When they returned the following week, Deborah Ann said, "It was difficult for me to shift from wanting to be his number one customer all the time. But I did stay focused on language that specifically describes what I want. My more realistic desire was for Chris to demonstrate to me that I am as important to him as his work. I want him to be more emotionally available so that I feel like I am the most important person in his life. I want him to demonstrate that I'm really, really important by treating me like I'm his number one customer, and for both of us to come up with the same definitions regarding what that means."

"I know," Chris replied softly. "You *are* number one with me. I realize you don't feel it."

She added, "I just need you to put me ahead of your work sometimes or maybe as important as your work—not all the time, just sometimes."

Forge the Golden Keys: Ask for What You Want

Jesse asked Deborah Ann to put her desire into three requests—three behaviors that would demonstrate that Chris put her first.

"I tried to follow the guidelines you gave me to make sure that what I want was specific, positive, present tense, measurable, time limited, and so forth," began Deborah Ann. "My first request is that for the next three months you be on time for our date night," she read. "If, on a rare occasion you are going to be more than three minutes late, I want you to give me a call at least 30 minutes beforehand." She paused as Chris repeated what she read.

"My second request is, for the next three months, I want you to treat me like your number one customer by putting our time together on the calendar just like you allocate time to your customers, business meetings, and out-of-town trips." Again Chris repeated her request.

"My third request is for the next three months, I want you to initiate and take complete charge of our private time together. This includes you scheduling our appointment times together, putting thought and planning into the time we spend together, and arranging for the babysitter."

Chris was sitting next to Deborah Ann, eyes closed but with his head tilted toward her. He listened intently without speaking, except to repeat each request. He asked her to repeat them because he wanted to make sure he heard each request accurately. Then he closed his eyes and paused for about five minutes.

When he looked up at Deborah Ann, his forehead was wrinkled and he said, "I would rank each request as hard, hard, and hard. But, I love you, Deborah Ann, and I want to be with you. I know that doing any one of them would be a gift to you. I understand that I would benefit too because of what Melva and Jesse said about 'stretching to meet our partner's needs.' I do want to be better at this and make you happy. So, with that in mind, I have to pick one to give you as a gift, right?"

"Right!" she replied. She turned around to look into his eyes, and put both hands on his thigh.

"Okay," he said. "The hard one that I would give you as a gift is to call you 30 minutes ahead of time if I am running late. I will also try harder to call you during the day. I do make an effort to call you and let you know that I am thinking of you. In the past, I didn't know how important it was for you to get a phone call until you told me that just one phone call from me during the day makes such a big difference."

Deborah Ann was smiling with glistening eyes. She said softly, "Yes, you are right, it does. It doesn't count if it is your last phone call of the day, but if it was your first call, I would be thrilled."

Even though Chris could not agree to make his first call each day to Deborah Ann, he assured her that she would not be his last. It wasn't the phone call per se, but what it represented.

Melva reminded her, "Realistically, you may not always be the first call. However, you would probably be closer to the first call more often. Know that every time you invite Chris to call you first and he calls, you will feel like you are experiencing the fulfillment of a lifetime of yearning to be a priority with someone you love. You, too, are stretching into being clear about asking for what you want. That's a good thing."

Unlock the Golden Door: Identify the Positive Payoffs for Each Partner

Jesse reminded Deborah Ann and Chris that there was a payoff for Chris by giving his gift and also for Deborah Ann as she received it. He asked Deborah Ann what would begin to heal within her as she received this gift.

"When you call me once a day to check in and see how I am doing, Chris, I will feel like I am your number one customer who has value to you. I will feel closer to you and begin to heal my terror of your anger and also my feelings of loneliness, sadness, and abandonment--those awful feelings of being in our marriage by myself. My terror of those terrible arguments when we blow up at each other will heal. Your calls are like vitamin pills. They nourish my feeling of connection to you. Instead of getting upset with you because you are so busy and feeling like I am carrying the entire load, I'll appreciate your reaching out to me and that gift will make my day." She sat back in her chair.

Chris had already mentioned his payoff—he would develop relationship skills. Melva asked him to be more specific about that. Chris had been thinking about it and said, "Granting you this gift will help me to overcome my resistance to being on time and help me to remember how important you are to me. It will also increase my ability to feel more deeply connected to you."

The Same Situation: Two Different Realities
Chris's Side of the Story

Describe the Surface of the Conflict

Chris said, "I know I frustrate Deborah Ann because I'm a workaholic. I would be the first to admit it. I have a hard time shutting off work. I have a very demanding job and people calling me from all over the world who want my attention right now. My clients and Deborah Ann want me at the same time, and to me that is very frustrating.

"And then, even when I am with Deborah Ann, people at work do not know how to back off and chill. I remember once we were at the airport getting ready to depart for vacation, and my employees kept calling me on my cell phone. I told them, 'Look, I'm on vacation, I'm leaving now. You have to be a big boy and deal with this, okay?' That was the way I have to talk to some of my people. They are big babies."

Deborah Ann interjected, "They do not hear him."

Chris said, "Right! Nobody hears me. It is as though what I am telling them does not matter. It's amazing. The kids are the same way. They are demanding. What frustrates me is that at the end of the day I am asking myself, what's left for me?

"I try," said Chris, "to show Deborah Ann that she is number one. I even remind myself to call her in the middle of the day. I make an effort to do that, and at the same time I cannot seem to get enough done for myself. I have a hard time with this. My intention is to call her when I am at work. Sometimes I just can't do it until the end of the day.

"Then, there will be the complaint that there wasn't enough money or something like that, and it becomes my fault. If there's something wrong, I take it as my fault. I take it on. That is something I grew up with.

"So we get into these power struggles when Deborah Ann says her needs aren't met. I didn't call or I didn't do something with the kids. I'm like; 'I cannot do it, Deborah Ann.' I put in 12-hour days. I really try not to bring work home, to shut it off, but it gets frustrating."

Chris had his own take on this pattern that was frustrating Deborah Ann. As we had seen with other couples, his frustration was the mirror image of hers. Chris said his biggest frustration was Deborah Ann's being in a state of panic when he couldn't be available to her. He knew she felt lonely, but when she demanded time with him, he felt frustrated.

"I know that underneath it is the frustration that I'm doing my best and my best isn't appreciated. It seems like the times I am not feeling appreciated are the times Deborah Ann wants to give me a hug. I got to tell you, it is difficult to accept those hugs."

Chris continued, "Then I get to that point where I shut down emotionally. And when I shut down, I go to work. I can work 24 hours a day, seven days a week. I can go home and work. I know Deborah Ann really feels rejected, she feels bad. But when I am upset, all of the work I do helps me to cope. My mind is focused on the task at hand and I can block out my feelings. I feel in control of what's happening. We don't solve it, but I feel relieved when we go back to life as usual after things calm down. At other times those frustrating feelings turn into anger which builds up and I begin to feel out of control."

Melva asked Chris how he reacted when he got frustrated with her, especially when he felt out of control.

"First I get triggered. And when I get triggered, I feel frustrated. Then this frustrating feeling builds up. I get pissed and try to hold it in. Then I get real angry and yell. And before I know it, I just blow up."

Deborah Ann added, "I mean, he really blows up."

"I go into a rage," Chris said. "And I punch things. I hit the walls. I become a rage-alcoholic and get downright ugly. I don't like that kind of reaction because it reminds me of what I grew up with."

Dig for the Deeper Feelings

What Was the Hurt Below the Anger?

We didn't want Chris to spend too much time talking about his reaction. We wanted him to go back to what happens before he blows up. Back to feeling that he is trying hard to please Deborah Ann but feels unappreciated. We both knew there was a deeper hurt. He too, had explored the deeper feelings beneath the surface of his rage.

"You know," Chris said, "I have been putting most of my energy into trying to manage my anger and rage that I have less energy left to think about the hurt. I guess this is something I don't even want to think about. I have told Deborah Ann over and over again that I want to be acknowledged when I do follow through on what she wants from me. All I hear is her criticism. So, I guess the hurt is from getting the criticism and not getting acknowledgment or appreciation when I do follow through." He paused for a moment. "I knew I was angry about this, but I didn't realize I was hurting so much."

What Was the Fear Below the Hurt?

Jesse expressed our curiosity about the fear beneath Chris's hurt. Chris looked away for a moment and then responded. "You are taking me to real foreign places. Fear? What could I be afraid of? I keep telling you that I get angry."

"Okay," Melva said. "Would you want to experiment with a guided imagery to get in touch with any fear you may have underneath your hurt?"

"Okay," he said, "but I'm not sure it's going to work."

This wasn't unusual for some who do this work with us. But we both knew Chris might have more success with this step with a little help. Jesse reminded Chris that not everyone is visual. Some are able to access their feelings or needs through their sense of hearing, others with feelings. So, Jesse guided him through an exercise to imagine identifying what would be the worst possible catastrophe he could experience if he continued to be criticized, unacknowledged, and unappreciated for the next few years.

Halfway through the guided imagery, tears began to flow from Chris's closed eyes. Jesse continued. When the guided imagery session was complete, Chris kept his eyes closed for a few minutes. When he opened his eyes, he didn't speak; he just looked at Deborah Ann.

"I know what the fear is," he said, almost inaudibly. "My fear is of not being competent enough to please you and take care of you, Deborah Ann."

The room was silent. He reached over to hold her, and sobbed aloud.

What are Your Memories of Similar Hurts and Fears?

We knew we could go deeper, and from the energy of his sobbing we thought he was ready to connect his present feelings to the past. Melva said to Chris, "From what you told us earlier, you felt this hurt and fear before you met Deborah Ann.

"Yes," he said quietly.

"Tell us about your memories of those feelings."

"This is something else I don't like to think about."

Jesse assured him that making this connection would be helpful to him and to Deborah Ann. It would help them to understand his contribution to the core of their conflict.

Chris took a deep breath. "I know you are right because I saw and heard what happened with Deborah Ann. I think I keep ignoring these feelings because I know what they remind me of. I also grew up in a household with a father who had a volatile temper and was emotionally and physically abusive. Both of my parents were cold and distant. The only time my dad and I ever really connected physically was when he was beating me with his fist, shoes, or whatever. He was always violent with my brother and me. We were punched in the head, hit with a shoe, and smacked. I was constantly being told, 'Shut the hell up,' 'Wise the hell up,' 'How could you be so stupid?' or "Come over here, asshole.' I also had the added distinction of being called the idiot or the kid with the big green teeth. He would not call me by my name. I could tell you countless stories." Chris was talking louder and faster. Melva asked him to take a few deep breaths and get centered before he continued. Chris had a tear in the corner of his left eye.

He straightened his posture before going on. There are more tears. He hesitated, and then continued. "I could tell you countless stories of my overwhelming need to please my father and the fear that he would not love me if I didn't do everything he wanted. He demanded so much of me. I felt incompetent. I was never given credit for what I did right. That really hurt." He started coughing.

"Are you okay?" Deborah Ann asked. "Would you like some water before you proceed?"

"That's a good idea," he replied, and we took a fifteen minute break. Then, looking at the floor, Chris continued. "I remember the closest thing to a holding and loving touch I got from my father was when my brother got killed. I was 32 years old. 32 years old! That's when he hugged me."

Like Deborah Ann's mother, Chris's mom used him as her confidant. "She would constantly pull me aside and say to me, 'I need someone to talk to. Your dad does not listen to me; someone has to listen to me.' She just pulled me in. My brother would escape, he would go down the street, and I would be left home, taking care of mom. The unspoken message I got was that my mother was demanding that I listen to her and take care of her.

"I can remember a time when she ironing and was weeping and wailing. She said, 'you're the only one here, you've got to talk to me, blah-blah-blah. I've got all these problems, but you're too little, I shouldn't be sharing all of this with you, but I have to talk to somebody.' So I just sat there and listened. But I was getting sucked into that black hole. Taking care of Mom was my job. It was so ingrained into my nature. I didn't like it then and I don't like it now."

Chris's voice was rising. He was getting angry again. Melva asked him to pause again and take more deep breaths, which he did.

"The upside of this," he said, "is that it did make me a good listener. That's where I learned how to take care of women because I could listen to their problems. But the downside was I was getting sucked into a black hole by having the job of taking care of mom. There was no tender holding or hugs from my mother. If she did hug me, it was a setup. It was very confusing."

Find the Gold Nugget: Identify Your Wants and Desires

Jesse didn't want to interrupt Chris's story because it often took time to go deeper, beyond his anger to what he truly needed.

He asked Chris what he wanted from his parents that he never got. He was clear about his answer immediately. He wanted both parents to tell him and show him that they loved him and that he didn't have to earn their love. He wanted them to acknowledge his need to be addressed instead of being a sounding board for his mother. He also needed for his father to appreciate him for what he did right and to express love instead of rage. He wanted to be treated like a valuable human being and to be assured that he was wanted.

Like Deborah Ann, Chris had a wound from not receiving something essentially nurturing in the form of socialization messages and experiences in childhood for who he was, versus how his parents wanted him to be as a perfect confidante or achiever. We asked him to shift from what he wanted in the past to what he wanted now from his wife.

"Chris," Melva said, "This is the perfect time for you to identify your global desire from Deborah Ann so that you don't continue to relive that pain. Think about and make the most outrageous desire that you can think of. If you could have anything you want, what would it be?"

"I know what I want," Chris said immediately.

"You do?" Deborah Ann said, sounding surprised.

"Yes, I do. My global desire," said Chris, "is for you to tell me every time I see you or talk to you what you notice that I do right and how much you appreciate me for doing it. I also want you to give me the freedom to have as much time as I want for myself and to encourage me to have time-out periods as long as I want. Instead of my running around taking care of everybody else, I want to sit down and chill out, without anyone, including you, asking me for anything. Only ask me what *I* want and need. Yeah! That's my global desire. That's what I want."

We watched Chris savor his feelings and waited before asking him to identify a more realistic desire.

"From Deborah Ann's experience," Jesse said to him, "you know there is one more step. Now we would like for you to make a more realistic request."

"I know," Chris said. He had been thinking about his more realistic request, and in fact he had written it down. He took out his folder, looked at it, and then at Deborah Ann.

"I want you, Deborah Ann, to understand that I need to be taken care of as much as you do. I need the same thing from you that I needed from my parents and never got. For you to listen to me and to acknowledge and appreciate what I do right, instead of criticizing me"

"I try to do that," Deborah Ann said.

Melva gently reminded Deborah Ann that she was now a safe container for Chris and how important it was for him to express his message completely before she responded.

Deborah Ann, first looking at Melva and then looking apologetically at Chris said, "Oh, that's right. I think I was beginning to panic. Thanks for keeping me on track."

Chris continued. "That's it; I really want to have time to be taken care of in those ways."

Forge the Golden Keys: Asking For What You Want

It was time to identify how he wanted the care, acknowledgement and appreciation with three specific requests. But he wanted to stop. He felt he'd accomplished a lot, so we told him that we'd continue the following week.

When they returned, Chris was ready. "I have three requests," he said, and proceeded to describe four healing behaviors that would replace Deborah Ann's panic and her demands that he spend time with her. The behaviors would indicate to him that she understood that he needed to be taken care of as much as she did.

"My first request," he said directly to Deborah Ann, "is for the next 30 days, I want you to calm down first, put your frustrations in perspective, and figure out how our time together can include you taking care of me." Deborah Ann repeated his request.

"My second request is that for the next 30 days you take time to think through your frustration with me and then get clear about and ask me for what you want from me, instead of complaining about what you do not like. Then acknowledge me when I do it."

Deborah Ann's eyebrows rose, but she remained silent until he finished speaking and then she repeated his words back to him.

For his third request Chris said, "For the next 30 days, I want you to think about and share a positive outcome that you would desire from me and then to relax and trust that it will happen." And finally, Chris said, "For the next 30 days, I want you to give me positive feedback, recognition, and appreciation when I follow through on giving you what you want from me."

"I am going to try all three," Deborah Ann said. "This was the clearest you have ever been, Chris. Okay, for the first request, calming down and thinking through my frustration without dialogue first will be hard for me because when I am angry I need to talk it through first. Then I can figure out how to take care of you. It would be extra hard if I don't feel taken care of.

"Your second request is also hard for me, to figure out what I want from you before we dialogue because it is through dialogue that I figure out what I want. The part about giving you positive feedback, recognition, and appreciation is between easy and hard, because sometimes it takes you a long time to follow through."

"Your third request," she said, "is easier for me to think about, but the second part of your request is extra hard."

Deborah Ann finished by saying that she was going to choose number 2, granting him the gift of figuring out what she wanted before dialogue, and also giving him positive feedback, recognition, and appreciation when he followed through on his promises.

Unlock and Open the Golden Door: Identify the Positive Payoffs for Each Partner

As Deborah Ann followed through on giving Chris her gift, healing would begin. But when asked what exactly would heal within him, Chris wasn't sure.

Deborah wanted to grant Chris the gift of giving him positive feedback, recognition, and appreciation about what he promised to do. Although Chris wasn't clear about how Deborah Ann's new behavior would provide healing for him, he was open to the idea that there was a connection to unresolved childhood experiences. He was able to make a connection about how this behavior would reduce his fear of failure in their marriage. He could imagine a future feeling of competence.

She had been aware of what she wasn't getting from Chris. However, she was clear that she would have difficulty remembering to acknowledge the ways he was successful.

Deborah Ann reminded him of what he had said earlier about his childhood experience.

"Oh yeah," he said. Then he turned to us and asked if this healing idea was really accurate. Jesse told him that we wanted him to identify the possibilities and then experience them, so that he would be able to answer that question for himself.

"Okay," he said. "Actually, I have thought about this. My first thought is that I believe that when Deborah Ann gives me this gift that it will help me to heal my fear of failure and incompetence as a husband and I will feel more valued and competent. I'll feel as if a weight has been lifted from my shoulders because I'll feel like I am valuable to you." His face showed relief. "Deborah Ann, this is really important for me."

Deborah Ann was visibly touched. Tears slowly flowed from her eyes and she smiled at the same time, while making eye contact with Chris. "I get it now. I get you now."

It was the first time she really understood how he struggled with a feeling of failure. "I had never thought of us as a failure," she said. "I love you and want more of you. Maybe I don't tell you enough about what you do that hits the bull's-eye for me. I now know I need to let you know. I also know that understanding is one step. The next step is following through and following through is where I will grow. Every time I follow through with this behavior I will stretch and grow more into the wife and companion you need me to be. I have to admit that before I started doing this couples' work with the two of you that I didn't know that I could request things from Chris and that he would respond positively. It had not dawned on me that I even had the right to ask him for what I wanted. That was what the growth was for me. This is enlightening for me."

She turned to Chris. "I have to remind myself that every time I asked you to make me your number one customer, you did your very best to give me that. I have to be mindful of noticing the steps you take to follow through, small and large. I will pay attention to your intent and your efforts, which means that there will be times that if you cannot give me exactly what I ask, you do give me what you can. I cannot tell you how wonderful this feels."

Melva said how important it was that Deborah Ann understood the efforts Chris had made.

Chris continued, "Although I have not been perfect, there have been times that I have demonstrated how I have tried to please you. I just need to feel that you are trying to please me in these important areas. You already do an outstanding job taking care of our home and family, and in so many ways you take care of me. I just need this important part as well."

Deborah Ann became tearful and said, "Yes, I know he loves and cares for me."

Chris, in a gentle voice, said to Deborah Ann, "You know, I get it! It was a deep childhood thing for both of us. We share similar childhood wounds. Our parents didn't meet our emotional needs. Neither one of us was honored or treated fairly. Both of us have been reliving our pain with each other. I understand my pain and yours. I cannot feel your pain, but I have compassion and empathy for it. I can see how doing this process together is helping us to grow together to have the kind of love and lives we both deserve. We are a work in progress. At times, it may seem like we are taking baby steps, but no matter how small, they are steps in the right direction." We watched the two of them embrace and share their heart-to-heart connection.

We also added that at times it would seem like one or both partners were taking baby steps, and that it was so important to acknowledge that no matter how small the steps were, they were steps in the right direction.

Asking for Change

It is of critical importance that couples learn the significance of reliving the painful relationship experiences of the past within their current relationships. Chris and Deborah Ann were a case in point of how devastating a relationship can be when frustrations escalate to anger and then into rage, instead of pinpointing exactly what goes on beneath the surface, where both partners are feeling so vulnerable and reacting from a place of survival. Couples need a safe environment of hearing the facts of each other's reality with understanding and compassion. Within that context each can ask for what is usually hidden beneath the conflict that they really want from the other, in order to feel loved and cared about.

Following through is what leads both partners to the level of reconnection and intimacy that they desire.

Where They Are Now

Some months later we checked in with Chris and Deborah Ann to find out how things were going. Chris began by saying that it had taken a lot of work to reach the point that they were at, a whole lot of work.

"We had to unmask the feelings beneath our pain and just keep working at it. Now we feel healthier and our bond is stronger. We're listening to each other and really hearing each other."

Deborah Ann said, "I feel that as we progress in our marriage, we are learning more and more how to communicate. It's baby steps because now that I am getting more of what I want from Chris, I sometimes have difficulty taking it in. I guess that I also have that feeling of not being good enough, which is another area of stretching and growing for me."

Chris said, "I feel that we are working together. I was resistant, at first, to following through on my commitment to give Deborah Ann the gift I promised. I did it anyway, although there were times I was frustrated with her. So the other night, I became angry. But I calmed myself down and articulated to Deborah Ann what I desired. She responded by actually giving me what I asked for, and that was so freeing for me."

"I believe," said Deborah Ann, "that Chris and I are starting to understand what it was we both need. Although we still get frustrated at times, both of us are able to articulate better. It has been slow. It does not happen all at once. It takes time and practice."

"We have grown a lot," said Chris. "I learn a lot from Deborah Ann when she gets upset with me. I am getting better at managing my natural inclination to jump in and defend myself. I have learned to ask Deborah Ann how she feels when she is upset. I am starting to realize what Deborah Ann had been pointing out to me. She tells me, 'You're running away here, what's going on?' Then I realize that this is my escape and I really have to focus on not avoiding the subject, but getting back into focus. I withdrew with drugs and alcohol; and I choose not to do those anymore. Now, it is the workaholism addiction I want to overcome.

"I am learning how to share myself: my goofiness, my seriousness, my artistic side, my analytical side, my happy side, my angry side, all parts of me, and not be ashamed. That is the beauty of it. I can be who I am."

Chris spoke of Deborah Ann with pride. "She works very hard. She is a good mother for our children, and a terrific woman to be with. I love her for that. I am glad I married her."

"Me too," Deborah Ann said.

CHAPTER 7
ROBIN AND MIKE'S STORY
RECONCILABLE DIFFERENCES

"Why Won't You Dance with Me?"

Robin, an African American woman, and Mike, her Caucasian husband, had been married for ten years. They sat close to each other, smiling and joking as they listened to stories from other couples we had worked with over the years.

Robin was warm, energetic, and friendly, with a soft and vibrant presence. Fashionably dressed in a comfortable, stylish dress that flattered her figure, she described herself as one who loved to socialize and had a wide range of interests, including dance. When we first met her, she immediately engaged us in conversation.

Mike was tall and slender, with medium brown hair. He smiled easily. Dressed comfortably in a light blue shirt and khaki slacks, he appeared somewhat reserved at first, but was very approachable and showed plenty of interest in others.

We asked about their attraction to each other. Robin was first to respond: "When we first met, I wasn't looking for love or intimacy. I'd decided that I had enough of that. My philosophy at that time was a live-and-let-live kind of thing.

"So our relationship started out as a casual friendship at work. For me it was a pleasant experience, being able to have long talks with Mike and laugh at his jokes. To me, it was clear that friendship was as far as this was going to go.

"Then we actually had our first date. It went so well, I was pleasantly surprised. My thinking was, 'Well, this is even better. Now I have a friend at work I can date. I'm very comfortable.' But I still wasn't looking for romance. Then one day, love showed up. Well, as I think about it now, I realize love didn't just show up; it developed from our ability to talk to each other. What a surprise that was!"

Mike had listened patiently to Robin, his arm around her shoulder, waiting for her to finish. "I wasn't looking for intimacy either. More than anything else, I was probably looking for someone to like me. I'd broken up with my first serious girlfriend probably about four or five months before. That was tough, and after that, I was still licking some wounds.

"Then I met Robin, and a friendship developed, for which I was really grateful. It was a steady, gradual, and effortless getting-to-know-you process. We spent endless hours on the phone, talking about just anything. Not about the big, dark secrets of our lives or anything like that. But I felt so close to Robin, and just couldn't do that with a lot of people."

Robin sat up in her chair and looked at us before she added, "Before we got married, we went out with each other for five years so I never sensed that love-at-first-sight feeling. It felt comfortable from the start. That confused me, because I was so used to drama. After a few years, there still weren't any screams or threats. It was really different! I decided I really liked it and would try it, because I had tried all the rest.

"I was very careful not to reveal too much about myself that could be detrimental, harm me, or be used against me in any way. Mike hadn't yet passed the time-tested mark, so I was still keeping him at a superficial level. Even though we had good times and connected very well, I was really kind of frightened by the idea of love. But I was very comfortable with what we had. It wasn't love, but it sufficed. Two years passed, then three. Everyone started asking me, *Well, how are you and Mike getting along?* 'Fine,' I'd say. 'We get along fine.' We *did* always get along fine."

"At the point he asked me to marry, I knew what we had was deeper than a close friendship because I had told him deep, dark secrets that no one else could know. It took five years for me to feel free enough to tell him all the really bad stuff I felt and thought. But he was still there. He'd stood the test of time. I could admit to myself that I felt more than friendship. I think that was when our relationship's romantic stage began."

"For me," Mike said, "our romantic stage began five years before we got married, because at that time, we were really carefree. I agree with Robin that our long talks about each other developed into serious talks about the future of our relationship. It seemed to develop slowly and naturally."

From Romance to Frustration

"After we married," Robin continued, "my lifestyle didn't change. He'd known me for five years and knew what I did, all the activities I thrived on. I really am an activities fanatic. As soon as one thing's finished, there are two others to come. It's like, with the whole world out there, I want to know it all. I want to do everything, and I want to feel everything. Mike wasn't like that. He didn't exercise, he wasn't a joiner, and he didn't have all these groups trailing behind him. His life was orderly—he got up, went to work, and came home. And he did that really well.

"After a while, my mother told me she'd noticed something about the two of us that troubled her. She said, *'You're going to have to change, Robin. You can't do all those things you like to do anymore.'*"

"What things?" I said in defense. "I don't drink and I stopped smoking. I don't go out too much."

"Mother said, *'You are going to have to stop being so busy with all these activities and start paying more attention to your husband.'*"

Her statement surprised me because she wasn't the domestic type. She had many outside activities and was a self-professed 'non-men' woman. After I thought about her words for a moment, I think I snapped back, 'Like you?'

"And she recoiled, *'Yeah, but I'm not married. You got married, so you're going to have to change.'*"

"I didn't want to hear this, so I kept doing what I loved. However, as time passed, I noticed how Mike seemed a little distant and I realized my mother was right, so I started to settle down. I stopped doing all the stuff I usually did. I stopped exercising, stopped leaving work and going to my fitness class and reaching home about nine or 10 o'clock. I would come home right after work and watch TV with Mike. That's pretty much what we did. Adapting was hard, but in the beginning, I liked it. And Mike seemed to love it.

"After a while, though, I started feeling constricted. That feeling got worse and worse. After a couple of years, it got so bad that I just decided, 'I'm not going to sit down on the couch and watch TV any longer.' I was gaining weight, as much as 10 pounds. I would complain to my friends and people at work and they would say, *Oh, that's marriage weight*, like it was some sort of marital penalty.

"I decided I didn't want the penalty. I needed to lose that weight, so I got more active again. It took me about three years to completely lose those ten pounds, and, during those three years, Mike started feeling neglected once more.

"Initially it was very difficult for me to express my frustration and inner conflict with Mike because of he was such a generous caregiver to me. As a matter of fact, in our relationship, the caring probably comes a lot more from him to me, than from me to him. He takes good care of me in wonderful, basic ways.

"So sometimes it was difficult for me to bring up the topic of doing the activities I loved to do away from home, like going out dancing. This issue was big for us, because I love to dance, and Mike doesn't. Dancing socially is difficult for him. For me, it's basic. Not something I like to just do occasionally. I have at least one night of the week when I go out to dance. It's a time for me to talk and laugh with friends. I like getting dressed-up, putting on perfume, fixing my hair, and all of that."

For Robin: Digging Beneath Surface Frustrations

Describe the Surface of the Conflict

Robin went on to explain how their different feelings about dancing became a source of her frustration because it was an important part of expressing herself and she was suppressing a very important part of her.

"After 10 years, I began to have a horrible feeling that I was so shut down that I'd forgotten how to dance because I hadn't done it in such a long time. So after years of not dancing, my frustration began to build. I decided that at that point in my life, I wasn't going to deny myself what I like. I decided to go dancing, even if Mike didn't. I was even prepared to dance with another man if I had to. Then I realized that would be disrespectful to my husband. But I did believe that once or twice a year, I should get out there and shake my bootie all night long. On those occasions when Mike did go with me" she continued, "we only stood around because he didn't like to dance and I didn't want to make him."

Robin said that about her only option for getting out on the floor was when *The Hustle* came on. That, Robin said, "was for those single women, when they get to dance because nobody else asked them. You know what I mean?"

The issue of their differences, Robin's need to be outside the home with him and Mike's need to be at home with her, was more about her need to express herself through that way, and his aversion to it. When her frustrations and Mike's reaction to them became overwhelming, they decided to try counseling and scheduled sessions with Melva.

"The counseling helped me to put my frustrations into a language Mike could hear. I began to say things like, 'I feel frustrated when I ask you to do something with me and you don't do it.' And I could continue to describe how it affected me, and explain what I needed. When we attended the weekend workshop I was able to give Mike even more information."

Melva asked Robin to describe her frustration a bit more.

"Well, Mike, dancing is important to me. And when I ask you to join me and either you say *no* or you say *yes* and don't participate, I feel frustrated."

"That was clear and descriptive." Melva continued, "What are the feelings that bubble up when you feel this frustration?"

Without hesitation, Robin responded, "I feel angry, discounted, and ignored. There are probably more, but I am most aware of those feelings." She sighed and sat back in her chair.

"That was also a clear description," Jesse told her.

Robin knew the next layer of the process, so she was ready to tell Mike how she reacted when she felt frustrated. "I react by what Mike might call nagging. But I don't call it nagging. I call it a reminder. I remind you, Mike, that you made a promise to me and broke it. When I remind you and you get upset, I also give you the silent treatment."

Dig for the Underlying Feelings

Melva asked Robin if she was ready to probe for some of her deeper feelings beneath her reaction.

Robin glanced to one side, paused for a moment, and said, "This is new to me—for someone to ask or care about what I'm feeling."

Jesse told her that her feelings were important, just as she was important. Robin turned and looked squarely at us, as if checking out whether she could believe us.

"Yes, Robin," Jesse repeated, "your feelings are important, just as you are important." She became tearful, and her facial expression showed that she was deeply touched.

Melva said, "When you react this way, I imagine you are reaching out to Mike. And underneath your reactive reaching out, it is clear to me that you may be feeling hurt. Will you tell Mike about what hurts you? This issue is deeper than needing to go dancing. Dancing represents something to you that Mike is still learning to understand more profoundly and therefore, hasn't yet validated. What is that hurt?"

Robin paused, and then said in an almost angry tone, "What hurts is that getting out of the house to go dancing means so little to Mike that he doesn't understand that I've given up a very important part of me. I guess you could say that my core hurt is that I feel the longer we're married, the less you hear and understand me. You put up a shield and what I'm trying to say to you, you call nagging. It's like you're saying, '*She's talking again, so maybe I'll just put up this shield.*'"

"I keep saying, 'You didn't listen to me.' That's how I know we're really married—'cause now he isn't listening to me. It's a big change from the past, when he hung on my every word and wrote me letters."

"Mike isn't listening to what dancing and other ways of expressing yourself means to you the way he used to," Melva repeated to her, "and that hurts. What scares you most, if you picture this continuing for the next year, five or 10 years?"

At first Robin wasn't able to name her underlying fear. Instead she talked around it, focusing again on Mike.

"What scares me is that after 10 years, Mike will not be able to break through his terror enough to hear me and meet me half way. What scares me more is I will get to the point that I will really disrespect him. I know you're not a weak man, Mike; I've seen you just plow through things that other people wouldn't even attempt. So I ask myself, what are you made of? Dancing isn't going to kill you."

Jesse asked Robin to focus on her own feelings and to describe to Mike her fear, if his behavior continued. She paused a moment to get in touch with her fear, then replied.

"I'm afraid that you won't take that step to be with me in a connected way. What scares me most is feeling ignored and being needy."

Then we knew she'd connected with her actual fear. Hearing the energy in Robin's voice, we felt it was time to go deeper to similar hurts and fears from her past history.

We gave Robin time to be with those feelings before proceeding. She looked down for a while, in deep thought. Then she straightened her dress, cleared her throat, and said she was ready.

Melva gently inquired, "What does your fear of being ignored and needy remind you of, from back before you met Mike?"

Robin's lips began to quiver. She was clearly fighting to hold back tears and appeared to be holding her breath. We waited and told her to breathe. Robin would start to talk and then stop. After several attempts she said, "I have a lot of memories of being ignored and feeling needy. Like the time I almost drowned, and my mother criticized me. I was in a city pool with a neighbor lady who had eight kids. I couldn't swim, and kids were horsing around. So I nearly drowned. The lifeguard got me out, but I went into shock. All the time I was thinking, 'I really can't go to the hospital because, boy, Momma's really going to be mad.' But because it was a city pool, and there was liability and whatnot, we had to go to the hospital.

"I needed compassion, but she didn't show any. I got criticized for something I had no control over. What made it worse was when my mother arrived at the hospital, she ignored me and started comforting the neighbor lady who took us swimming, who was hysterical. I needed her comfort. Instead, when our neighbor lady tried to apologize by saying, *Oh, I'm sorry, I almost let your child drown,* my mother's reply to her was, 'That's okay, these things happen.' I couldn't believe it. I needed her to comfort me like she'd comforted our neighbor. But she came over to me and said angrily, 'Get up; there's nothing wrong with you. We don't have any money for any doctor visits.' I hated that. I felt embarrassed to be there. My worst fears were realized. My mom was mad at me."

Robin continued and described how situations like that had taught her not to need anything from anybody. "Not that my mother wasn't able to be supportive and compassionate. But she *chose* not to be supportive and compassionate with *me*. I could see the disparity."

Intense feelings showed on Robin's face and in her angry, almost enraged words. But beneath this intensity, we sensed tremendous hurt and pain.

After that incident, Robin said, was when she decided "to carve a moat around myself. It was my message to the world that I didn't need anyone because invariability, they would disappoint me."

To make matters worse, Robin said, her mother went around helping people whom she thought needed her. But to Robin, she said, "You were very strong, you never needed me."

"She really didn't understand that I *had* to be strong," Robin told us. "I didn't have any other support. I decided that she treated me that way because I wasn't likable and that it had to be me, because she was nice to everybody else."

Robin reported that much of the time, her stepfather didn't show compassion either. "He'd had an atrocious upbringing, and he passed that along. His way of teaching me things was to be intentionally cruel. He'd say, *The world is a hard place. You might as well start learning about it now.*"

Identify Your Wants and Desires

"Listening to your history," Melva said, "it is clear that being invisible so you didn't feel the pain of not feeling acknowledged or valued, helped you to survive emotionally. It is also clear that it was out of the question to ask your mother and stepfather for what you wanted. However, if you had the opportunity to ask for what you wanted, what would that have been?"

"That's a scary question because there is nowhere in my wildest dreams that I would have ever let myself know what I needed from them. However, since I did go through this process during counseling and the workshop regarding other issues I have, I know I wanted two things. The first thing I wanted was for them to acknowledge what was important to me. Now it is amusing for me to fantasize about that. That leads me to the other thing I wanted, which was for both of them to respond to me with understanding, empathy, comfort, and emotional support when I was hurt or scared. Whew! That's quite a mouthful."

Robin had made a connection between past and present. It was time to connect the dots. Jesse asked her to make a global desire request of Mike. Before speaking, Robin told us how important this step was for her. She said she needed to take her time, so we granted her wish.

Lost in her thoughts for what seemed to be about five minutes, Robin finally made eye contact with Mike.

"Mike", she said slowly, "my global desire is for you to feel that my needs are important to you all the time, including dancing. I want you to invite me to go dancing with you every week, and dance every dance with me." They both laughed "To tell you the truth, "Robin added, "I'd be so happy if you granted me that wish, but I know it's global."

"Yes, it is, "Melva agreed. "Take your time to savor that desire."

"I think I will," Robin said while smiling. "Oh, how wonderful that would be!"

After a few moments, Jesse interrupted her fantasy so that he could ask her to make her global desire more specific and realistic.

"More specific and realistic?" Robin asked. "Okay. I wrote it down and I am going to read it." Robin pulled a neatly typed piece of yellow paper from her notebook. She sighed, and then she read it aloud. "Mike, my realistic desire is, I want you to understand why it's so important for you to join me in activities I enjoy; especially dancing."

Melva asked, "Do you mean that one important way you will feel a deeper connection with Mike is through sharing activities like dancing?"

"I like the way you put it. Yes. That would happen if I got what I wanted. My companion would be *with* me, and we'd be doing something *together*."

Asking for What You Want

Robin had been clear about what she wanted from Mike. Now it was time for her to tell him *how* she wanted it: what behavior would let her feel visible, cared for and more deeply connected to him. She'd done her homework on this point, too.

"But," she admitted, "I had to do the exercise three times. Now I think I have it clear."

She turned to Mike, cleared her throat again, settled in her chair, and read her requests. "My first request is, for the next month, when I ask you to do something like going to a party and dancing, with me, you tell me straight whether you will or not. And if you say you will, then I want you to actually participate in the activity, like dancing with me.

"My second request is, for the next month, whenever you feel manipulated or unclear about my needs, ask me right away, *Is this what you really want?* Ask me if I am just making a general statement, or if I'm actually making a direct request for you to do something for me. That'll give me an opportunity to make it clear."

To clarify, Jesse asked her, "And how long is 'right away'?"

"The minute I say it, and he gets that feeling," she replied.

"And my third request is, for the next 30 days, I want you to hear me out by repeating back what I say I want. Tell me about how it makes sense to you and tell me what you imagine I'm feeling."

Mike interrupted. "Okay, Robin, I know why you're asking for this. Because when you say the same thing over and over, I step in and want to do something about it instead of just hearing you out."

"Yes," Robin asserted. "That becomes part of the problem. That's why I need you to follow through on this step."

It is now time for Mike to share with Robin the amount of stretching and growing that would take place with him in order to meet her needs. He had been listening intently, his facial expression changing with each request Robin shared. Mike understood that the next step was to rank each request as easy, hard or extra hard.

"Okay," said Mike, let's see. The first is hard. The third is also on the hard side. The second one—for the next month, when I'm feeling manipulated, used, or unclear about what you are telling me you need, to say so right away. Hmmm, that would be hard, just because it's not my way to deal with that stuff. But that's the one I'm going to pick."

Surprised, Robin asked, "You're going to grant me that?"

"I'm going to grant you that wish."

Jesse and Melva ended the session and gave the couple homework for the next week.

Identifying Positive Payoffs for Each Partner

Robin and Mike returned the following week, having spent their time thinking about what healing and growth would take place when Mike gave Robin his gift.

"It took time to think this through and remember the question Melva asked me about my hurt of feeling ignored, acknowledged and valued. Those feelings fit for me. Receiving your gift, Mike," she said, "will help me overcome my fear of being invisible and needy. It'll help me to feel safer to ask for what I need, especially when I don't want to do something by myself, for whatever reason, including dancing."

Jesse asked, "What other way will this affect you?"

"Oh, in lots of ways, especially feeling more worthy of receiving from Mike. I won't beat myself up and tell myself that I'm taking advantage of you, Mike. That will then free me up to do things for *you*, when you ask me, without feeling put upon.

"And," she added, "I'll know you thought enough of me to push through fears from your past that have really been locking you down. That level of confidence," she said flirtatiously, "is really sexy."

"I *like* that," said Mike, smiling. He then added, "I do want to break through this fear and give you what you want. I know this issue of our conflict about dancing has deep roots in childhood and your painful experiences with your mother and stepfather, and it is clearly connected. I know this is one of those times you get sick of bumping your head against the same old wall. I also know that granting you this gift will help me to grow. This will stretch me to overcome my inability to speak up for myself and say it if I think I'm being taken advantage of. Or to invite you to understand why dancing is so difficult for me. I've never been good at doing that, and committing to this should help me overcome my fears and terror."

Melva coached, "Do you see any other area of growth for you, Mike?"

Mike turned to Robin. "I was just thinking about something I've always tried to do, which is doing something for you simply for the joy it brings you. It helps me to be clear on what you want. When I know that, I very much enjoy the feeling that I get from providing it. But still I hear that little devil on my left shoulder, saying, *Remember to put this on your score sheet for when you want something down the road.* So that's one thing that I'm still working on— more of a sense of peace and just releasing the struggle over the whole thing.

"I think the most difficulty I will have in following through is feeling Robin's priorities will usurp mine—feeling that just my showing up isn't good enough. So I will also develop my ability to give without thought of getting some kind of reward in return."

The Same Situation: Two Different Realities

After a short break Jesse said to Mike, "It's your turn now."

"Oh, and am I ready for my turn!" Mike laughed. "You're right. There are two sides to every situation. I appreciate how you two helped me to stay focused on Robin and hear her out without interruption. I am looking forward to having the same experience with her."

Describe the Surface of the Conflict

"Robin was talking about changing her lifestyle from being so active to spending more time at home with me. It wasn't like I'd just been sitting home eating bon-bons. A big part of why I found myself at home a lot was because Robin takes after her mom. She's not a very domestic person. I like to have the house somewhat clean and organized, so I found myself taking care of our home by myself. I was doing the dishes, the laundry, vacuuming, and keeping house—not for me only, but for the two of us. That didn't really afford me a lot of time to get out, which I would have enjoyed doing."

Mike said that he and Robin "often butted heads over this, but never solved it. "We'd argue, make up, move on, but never really deal with it." We were both making compromises. Robin was staying home more than she liked, while I was going to more parties than I really wanted to, just because she wanted me to go. She was adapting and I was adapting. I don't know that either of us was really happy with our compromises."

Robin looked at him and interrupted, "You can only do it so long. It's not normal."

"Yeah," Mike responded, "that's why we're here."

Melva asked, "Since Robin brought up your conflict of dancing, will you describe your frustration with her and what is underneath it?"

Mike took a few minutes to explain why he hated dancing. "It has more to do with my past than with Robin. When I was a teenager, my sister used to sing in a band, playing the bar circuit. One time my whole family went out to one of these places to hear her sing. One of my sister's best friends was there, and the band started playing one of her favorite songs. At that point, I'd never danced before—at all. So what did my sister's friend do? She grabbed me and said, *'That's my favorite song. Dance with me.'*"

"Without waiting for my answer, which would have been, 'no way', she pulled me out on the floor. No one else was out there, just her and me and everyone else watching. I didn't know what in the world I was doing. Right away, I knew I didn't like it! When we sat down, I felt humiliated. I imagined that everyone was having a private chuckle, but no one was going to let me know that out loud."

"To make it worse, there was another time when I went to see my sister playing at this fancy hotel. As fate would have it, there was a female co-singer in her band. Again, my whole family went to see her. This woman sang a solo. The rest of the stage was blacked out, and the spotlight focused on her. She came over to the table, grabbed me, and wanted me to dance with her in the spotlight. I should have known there was going to be trouble. So, I though to myself, 'Here we go again.' So there I was, hating all of it, having made a mission to avoid it, and all I could think was, 'Oh, no! '"

"I panicked. I didn't do a good job. I stepped on her toes. Then I stepped on her dress. It was awful. I felt humiliated again. I resolved to never get on a dance floor again. Isn't it ironic that I fell in love with someone who loves to dance?" The worst part of his frustration, he admitted, was that Robin doesn't understand his terror of being humiliated again by dancing in front of people. "I feel so much pressure when you insist that I get out on the dance floor with you. I feel like you are demanding that I perform."

Jesse asked Mike what else he felt in addition to the humiliation and pressure.

"Inadequate!" Mike said full volume. "I get paralyzed. I freeze up and withdraw. You know, I get kind of testy. I go into the shell I built over the years and turn all those feelings inward. I won't communicate and won't express my real feelings. Obviously, that just creates more stuff to deal with later on."

What Hurt Underlies the Reaction?

We now had more information about what went on below the surface for Mike. His reaction made sense. There was more digging to do. He had already opened the door to describe his hurt, and since he had been through the process before, he knew the next step and spontaneously said, "What hurts the most is that Robin does not understand the pressure I feel dancing in front of others."

Like many men, Mike wasn't used to putting his feelings into words. But after listening to the other men in the group, he had begun to learn a new vocabulary of feelings, and so he was prepared to answer this important question.

"The hurt," he continued in a very low tone of voice, "was when I would bring up how difficult this was for me, and when you, Robin, could not seem to hear nor understand me.

"It's like she concentrates so much on what she wants and ignores what I need, almost as if I were invisible."

It was another good example of a partner expressing the other side of the couple's coin. They both felt the same mirror image of hurt from feeling invisible, unheard, and misunderstood.

"I know that the next question you're going to ask," Mike went on, "is about my fear. I'm ready to answer that one, too. My fear shows when I get the feeling of paralysis. Robin calls it stubbornness or resistance. She doesn't get it that the thought of dancing recalls all that stuff—embarrassment and humiliation from the past. It's unbearable! I know that more than anything, Robin wants me to break through that. And I want to break out of it, more than anything. But it's a struggle and it will take a safe, step-by-step process to get through it. We have talked about structuring it in a way that it could feel safe for me. We tried practicing at home, but although we had the best intentions, neither one of us ever really followed through sufficiently to do anything about it."

"Part of me wants to please Robin by dancing with her. The other part of me struggles with the possibilities of failure, humiliation, and maybe rejection, from all the other people who are there laughing at my expense."

From what we had already learned from Mike, we knew how such feelings connected with his past.

"I remember this childhood fear of failure to perform, failing and feeling humiliated. I also felt kind of ignored and invisible many times in my family, because when I didn't know how to do something, I was afraid to approach my parents." Mike explained that in his family, he could never draw attention to his own needs.

"With so much tension always going on between my alcoholic father and martyred mother, I was too afraid to bring up what *I* needed. They were always so close to the edge. I never knew how they were going to react. They were never violent or anything, they would just brush me off or snap at me a little bit—enough to reinforce that I wasn't significant enough for them to get past their issues and deal with me and help me. So that's how I developed a pattern of not wanting to share things that were troubling me, because I was afraid that they didn't want to know."

Mike said he had problems in school, starting in the fourth grade, but never felt like he could go to his parents about it. "I was just petrified of letting them know. Not that I feared what they would do. It was just the action of interacting with them that was a problem. I felt like they just kind of put me on autopilot. It was like they pointed me in the right direction and just let me figure it out for myself. So I was on my own. But I felt lost because I was too young for that."

Mike's tone changed and he became somber. He shifted his posture, staring down at the cup of coffee on the table in front of him.

After a few moments passed, Melva asked tenderly, "What was the worst feeling?"

"There were many worst feelings. I think the very worst was the fear."

"Would you tell us more about your fear?"

"Yes, as I think about it, maybe it was more like terror. I felt terror whenever I even thought about being vulnerable with my parents. It could be anything from revealing my troubles in school or having a crush on a girl that didn't pan out, or anything like that. And man, it was just horrible. I just couldn't do it. So I had to turn all that within and just kind of cope and figure it out by myself. My terror was that I would be rejected because I didn't feel important enough to matter. It was bad enough to come to them just about day-to-day kind of stuff. But if I came to them with a real need and they didn't meet it, that would have been a real kick."

Jesse was leaning in toward Mike and asked, "And that carried over?"

"Yes, it carried over into my relationship with Robin because I would have some of the same feelings. She would need to do her thing and her thing was difficult for me—but I had needs too, and I wasn't able to tell her what they were because of that fear of rejection. I also felt that my needs weren't important enough for her to change what she was asking me to do."

Identify Your Wants and Desires

Jesse coached Mike. "One of many ways intimacy skills are developed is when we experience receiving love and care in very specific ways. For instance, Mike, you talked about how difficult it was to approach your parents about what you needed. What was it that you wanted so much and never got?"

"I have thought about that a lot over these past several months. I think what I needed most was to hear them say they were interested in me and my life, including my struggles, and that they would help me through it all."

Mike was replaying the same kind of struggle with Robin. We were clear that he was in a place to ask for what he wanted.

"Think now about this issue of Robin wanting you to dance. What would your global desire be?" Jesse said. "Make sure what you want is drastic and dramatic. What do you want from Robin to replace her frustrating behavior of insisting that you dance?"

Mike looked down for a moment, and then looked up at Jesse and said, "I think my global desire, if I could ask for anything I want, would be for Robin to say to me 'Hey, I love you, and you never have to dance again. If you never dance again, I'll still be happy.' And then I would want for her to lavish me with affection and appreciation for not having to do it."

He was looking at Robin. She was smiling and so was he.

"Good job!" Melva exclaimed. "Enjoy that idea for a while." After a few minutes, Melva continued, "Now, would you make that global desire more specific and realistic? What specifically do you want from Robin to replace her frustrating behavior?"

"Oh, I know that one," Mike said. "I want support."

"Would you be more specific?"

"Well," Mike said, "I want you, Robin, to support me in joining you in activities, especially dancing, in a way that honors my vulnerability and need to feel important to you. That way I would not be so afraid."

"What do you mean?" Robin wondered aloud.

"I mean I want us to work out a step-by-step process to help me heal my terror and gradually give you what you want. I also have a desire for myself," he added, "which is to be able to break out of this and give you the joy of dancing with me. I want the freedom of breaking free of those fears."

Asking For What You Want

Mike's desire was clear. It is time for the how. Jesse asked Mike to think of three specific behaviors from Robin that would fulfill those desires.

Mike had done his homework, using the worksheets he had filled out during counseling sessions and the workshop. He asked Robin to turn and face him as he read his list. He also asked her to repeat each item on the list so that he knew she heard him. Robin agreed.

"One behavior I would like from you, Robin, is that once per week you indicate a joint effort. For instance you could say, 'I want to do this thing with you because I really don't want to do it by myself. Can we work on it together?'" Robin repeated it.

"The second request is, when I do participate, I want space to do this dance thing my way. I want this each time."

"The third behavior is for you to participate in a dance that you could do by yourself, like *The Hustle*."

Melva gave Robin the next step. "Okay, Robin, now you have heard and repeated Mike's requests for three possible caring behaviors. How would you rank them in terms of you stretching and growing to meet his needs?"

With her eyes fixed on Mike, Robin answered. "Well, all of them are a little difficult. So is there a time limit, or is this forever?"

Mike beamed. "Just for the next century. After that you can go back to step one." They both laughed.

Melva clarified. "Start off for the next 30 days at a time. Then review how you're doing each week and revise as necessary."

"I'm ready," Robin said. "Number one is pretty easy, and each time I want you to do something with me, I'll just say, *Hello!*

"Number two, as I think about it now is kinda medium, participating your way. But I can do that. And number three, to do some of the dances by myself. Well, you see, I don't want to do any by myself. I really kind of think you don't need number three."

"What does that mean in terms of ranking—easy, hard, or extra hard?" Jesse asked.

"Oh! That one would be extra hard, definitely."

Mike joined in. "I am not surprised. When I got to number three, I was thinking, 'I know she ain't going to pick this one.'"

"Yeah, well, I'll knock this out," Robin interrupted. "I probably wouldn't get to number three. But numbers one and two I think are doable."

"Okay, Robin," Melva added, "now you can select one behavior request. Just pick one of the three."

Robin thought for a moment. "I'll pick number one. Each time I want you to do something with me as a joint effort, I'll say to you, 'I would like to know if we can work on this together and follow through.'"

Identify the Positive Payoffs for Each Partner

Melva turned to Mike and coached him with the next step. "Will you look at Robin and complete this sentence? 'Thank you, Robin. Receiving your gift of telling me clearly what you want me to do with you as a joint effort will help me overcome…'

Mike answered slowly, "Thank you Robin. Working together as a joint effort will help me overcome… I think what it will help me overcome my feeling of the terror of being ignored and not feeling supported. Like how I get when I feel like I'm in the spotlight and under pressure to perform. I won't feel like I've got to take care of everything by myself with no help, like I did growing up. And knowing you are stretching to meet my needs is a message communicating I am worth direct feedback. That will help me to feel more adequate and I will feel safer to get through my terror to try something I am uncomfortable with. That will help to heal my childhood wounds."

"Good job, Mike. Tell Robin what you would be feeling instead of that terror, what you would be feeling instead?" asked Melva.

"Okay, what I'll feel instead is loved and supported."

They were almost done. It was then Robin's turn to reflect on how giving Mike this caring behavior would stretch her.

Robin was animated. "Okay, I agree to clearly state when I want Mike to join me in activities and give him time to take small steps his way. I'll remind myself that he has to take care of himself so he can give me what I need.

"So, granting you that gift, Mike, will enable me to grow and stretch into developing my ability to see the compassion and love you are showing me by trying. I will feel worthy of your compassion and of accepting your efforts to overcome your terror to please me." Thinking further, she added, "I will also stretch and grow beyond my reluctance to be known. And I'll learn to tolerate him saying 'no' without me interpreting it as rejection."

The Importance of Connecting Childhood Memories to Current Hurt and Fear

Mike and Robin were an example of how an issue that might appear to be superficial may have many layers of unfinished business at its core. The hurt, fear, and longing for reconnection in their present areas of discomfort were an example of how this often plays out in a committed love relationship. Both Robin and Mike could see how the ways they related to each other in the "here and now" were a repeat of other "deja vu" moments from their past—an instant replay of a core scene that both had lived over and over throughout their relationship history.

We saw how Robin's painful memory of the time she almost drowned, and how being a recipient of her mother's criticism instead of compassion, impacted her in her present-day life. Her mother had not developed the skills needed to nurture Robin's feeling of worthiness. When Mom was vulnerable she struck out to defend herself. To Robin, her early experience was that her mother was capable of being compassionate toward her, but that she chose not to be. Her mother's defensive reaction was an assault to Robin's self esteem. The belief that *it's got to be me, because she's nice to everybody else* is a child's way of trying to make sense out of pain. We also saw the decision Robin made at that early age to be strong for herself, because she didn't have any other support.

Being strong for Robin was a character trait that Mike adored during the romantic phase of their relationship. Predictably, that same trait later became interpreted as Michael feeling manipulated and used.

For Michael, the interaction process with Robin helped him to be more forthright when he was struggling with his terror. Her support led to a feeling of safety, because it was enough to enable him to push through the fears from his past that had been locking him down. An extra bonus was that his wife perceived his efforts as sexy.

Where They Are Now: An Update on Robin and Mike

Several months passed before we asked Mike and Robin for a report.

Mike spoke first. "The success part of this story is that I have really been focusing a lot on trying to push past my fear of walking onto the dance floor. Robin had been getting more insistent on me doing this, and it was having the wrong effect on me. However, I am taking small steps to get on the dance floor as an expression of loving and caring for her. It also makes me deal with and grow through my feelings of self-consciousness."

Robin added, "I really work hard to see and acknowledge his efforts."

"Yes she does, Mike said enthusiastically. "What I am most proud of is the ability I now have to tell Robin what I need as I take my small steps. Now I say, 'Look, what I really need from you right now is just support and direction—not telling my why it's silly to feel the way I do.' She hears me, and she is able to just said, 'Okay, let's go over here in the corner where no one will see us.' So we've done that and danced for a while. And I survived. We didn't have to call 911 or anything. You know, I was really glad to be able to do that for myself and for her. I'm hoping to build on that. I imagine that the next time it comes around, I might feel the tension return, but we have at least started the ball rolling."

Robin was listening and was ready to contribute. "When I first gave this gift to Mike, my internal experience was a feeling of resistance because I felt like I was bossing him around, a tendency I do admit I have. Then I discovered and was able to understand that he could say 'no' at any time, and that it didn't mean forever, it just meant not right then. Sometimes he postpones joining me because he just wants to get his mind and body together, and I can appreciate that"

"We've really progressed in other areas too," Mike added. "I remember the times I wanted to tell Robin what I was experiencing, and she would cut me off. We had to deal with a situation like that yesterday, because we had a disagreement about something, and I was trying to express what my feelings were. But every time that she felt like it was criticism of her way of thinking, she was right there to head it off. Usually I get only half a sentence out before she cuts me off. Yesterday, though, we were able to talk that one through. And we were able to understand where each of us was coming from.

"I have changed in terms of liking to talk things out, because now we know how and can see the benefits of doing that. I am able to express how I'm feeling and what my needs are and whatnot, and Robin is willing to listen to hear what I have to say. We've been through a lot, but now we're getting to the point where intimacy and deeper connection are really, truly possible. And it feels good."

Six years later, Mike and Robin became parents of a beautiful little girl.

CHAPTER 8
THEODORE AND NIA'S STORY
BUILT-UP FRUSTRATIONS AND RESENTMENTS

"How Could You Say You Love Me and Show up Late?"

"Theodore, I can't believe you are late picking me up again!" said Nia.

"What do you mean? I can't believe that you are raising your voice at me again!" Theodore snapped in return.

Theodore and Nia were an African-American couple in their late 30's. They had known each other since childhood and been married for 10 years.

Nia was a professional dancer, tall, lean, sculpted, vivacious, and poised. She walked with awareness and spoke as if she were reciting a poem.

Theodore was an engineer with a reserved manner until you got to know him. When he finally spoke to you, you discovered that he had been listening closely and had thoroughly thought through what he was going to say before responding.

Theodore and Nia did not have children and led very busy lives. She traveled nationally and internationally giving dance performances. He worked long hours. While they had very different and quite demanding jobs, they still found ways to support each other in their marriage and their professional lives. Most of the time, it worked for both of them.

Theodore and Nia sat side-by-side; turning toward each other as they took turns describing one of the frustrations they have not worked out to their satisfaction.

"You weren't so short with me in the beginning," Theodore said. "I was late before and didn't get this kind of reaction. How come that changed after we became an official couple?"

According to Theodore, when they first got to know each other they felt very close and had long conversations about many different things. "This never came up when we were talking about life, work, what we wanted to be, and what we wanted to do in life," he said. "I'm just thinking about those times when we shared our different perceptions. Our different points of view felt good."

Their Attraction

"So how did the two of you get together?" Melva asked.

Theodore looked into Nia's eyes and said softly, "I think I want to start."

"Okay, "she said.

"I met Nia at a young age," Theodore began. "And my first recollection of being attracted to her was almost ten years after we met. She was physically attractive, but what drew me to her the most was that I was able to have certain types of conversations with her that I had not been able to have with other women, about things I could only share with my closest male friends. Her female perspective fascinated me. She was a woman, yet her perspective was different from my mother's. I could talk to her, and she would listen and get a good take on where I was coming from. The more she listened, the more I was attracted to her.

"In retrospect," he added, "I realize that I didn't hear much about what was happening with her life because I was talking so much about what was happening in mine. Maybe I wasn't ready to listen to her, or maybe she wasn't being vocal enough to say, 'Theodore, shut up and listen to me.'"

Theodore said that their friendship developed until he knew he wanted a deeper relationship, but when he first told her that, she blew him off. "But we continued to talk about a lot of things, like who we were and what we were doing. There were a lot of things about my life that Nia had always known that no one else knew."

"And vice versa." Nia interjected. "Theodore was the one person who witnessed some of what was going down in my family. I didn't want to tell anyone about those things."

Theodore turned and looked at Nia. His eyes glistened. "All I could think about was how great it was being with this woman who wasn't only physically beautiful, but intellectually, spiritually, and mentally beautiful as well. Those were the qualities that were then and still are more important to me.

"What I was searching for in a mate was mutual sharing. What I thought I had to bring to a relationship was my ability to share. I knew that was unique because not all men share their emotions. I was fortunate to be the only male around a bunch of females, including a sister, three female cousins and aunts galore. I developed a perspective that most men don't have about dealing with women as a whole."

Before Nia and Theodore made a commitment, he had other dreams as well. Those dreams included his vision of himself being married and having the ideal family life. "I'm not going to lie. In my mind, I was looking forward to being home the same time during the week and eating dinner together every day like our family did while I was growing up. We had a pattern of sitting down at the dinner table together, enjoying family conversation. That became etched in my mind as, okay, this is what it's going to be like for me when I get married. And I was also looking for lots of touching, more touching than I saw with my parents. What I wanted most was a feeling of closeness through touching and holding. That's what I was looking for."

Theodore sighed and looked at Nia, who had been listening attentively and nodding from time to time. There was silence for a couple of minutes. Then Jesse said to her, "It's your turn, Nia."

"Yes, I know," she said. "It fascinates me to hear Theodore describe this. I can go way back to describe what I was looking for."

"When I thought about the kind of person that I wanted to spend my life with, I dreamed about the kind of man described in the lyrics of the 70s love songs. My family used to travel a lot at night. To entertain myself, I would channel-surf and listen to the radio. And I swear to God, since I'm such a quick study with learning lyrics, I could tell you every word to every song. I remember looking up at the sky and fantasizing about the romantic kind of love described in those songs. That wasn't the romance I saw with my parents. What I did see between them at times was just horrible. They didn't express the kind of affection that fit my picture."

"In my search, I developed a history of spending time going in and out of relationships. After years of trying, it became really, really clear to me that there was a lot I didn't know about creating the kind of romantic love I dreamed of. I did know that I didn't want to recreate what I had experienced in past relationships. I also didn't want the tension my parents had between them. I wanted a partner who would be part of a dynamic team—a team of partnership and openness. And in this partnership, I wanted more of a voice."

"I saw the two of us meeting the requirements of being a very dynamic team. Each of us had to feel whole within ourselves in order for our team to be successful. We knew that if either felt like they were taking a backseat, even if by choice, there would be a problem. So we decided that we wanted to circumvent that. We did this by building a deep level of communication between ourselves."

"We had the ability to speak very deeply about a number of things before we even became romantic. We knew each other so well that we were able to intuit certain things. It was just a kind of knowing, a deep sort of telepathic knowing. It's like I saw it coming." She turned to Theodore; "I heard it in your voice."

"I mean, our friendship was incredible," Theodore said. "We went through our 20s and didn't even think about being married. When Nia got to the point where she decided to be my life partner and was serious about getting married, we were in our 30s. I wasn't going to get married because I *needed* Nia. I wanted to get married to Nia because she complemented me and because I *wanted* to be with her. I didn't *need* to be married; I *wanted* to be married. And I wanted to be married to Nia."

From Romance to Frustration

Nia continued, "So we decided to get married. That's when the romantic stage began. I had to figure out my part in creating the romance. That started with the first time we spent the night together. What I remember most was the nightgown I bought that I knew you were going to see, Theodore. I remember when you asked me if I was going to stay the night, kind of thing?"

"Oh, yes, I remember clearly!" Theodore said with a wide smile.

"Then I told you that I would. So, I came over to your apartment and prepared to spend the night. I was a little confused about where my things were supposed to go—like my toothpaste, personals, and stuff. All that had to be figured out. You know, the nitty-gritty stuff that you don't go through with everybody.

"Then we got to the engagement part, which lasted a year. By then, my work required that we live in two different cities while we planned our wedding. We were immersed in a process of researching and figuring out all the details because we wanted a meaningful ceremony. For instance, Theodore wanted our rings made out of solid gold because nobody else was doing that. We wanted to think through our rituals because we wanted them to be special. The flashes of those memories I have are awesome."

"We had our tense times, too. We had two big decisions to make—about the name I was going to use and where we were going to live. I decided to keep my name rather than hyphenate it or use his. I was living and working in Washington, D.C., and wanted Theodore to move there. His concern was that if he moved where I was, he would be alone because he didn't know anyone there. He asked what he would do when I was on the road. My response was, 'You make a life. You meet a few people.' I was kind of pissed at the fact that I had to deal with it."

"It turned out really quickly that I was going to be the one to move. Things just started to fall apart for me where I was. So I decided I was going to go to Michigan. And I had to cleanly cut the rope from what had been my support system before going to the Midwest. I was suddenly in business for myself. I had to make new friends. I had no idea what was going on with the feminist movement in Michigan; I didn't know what the artistic community was like. I didn't know what Detroit was like, and what I'd heard wasn't very positive.

"So, I moved to Michigan and moved in with Theodore. The next thing we had to face was negotiating our lifestyles. When we lived apart, our lifestyles were basically the same. After I moved in with Theodore, my lifestyle changed. I realized that I would be working a whole lot more after we got married than I had prior to that."

Theodore joined in. "Yes, the change for us began the first month or so after Nia moved in, when we were home together. We started to deal with my work schedule. Through the whole period that we dated, we never had to see each other every day. We were always doing something fun. Then, when we started living together, we started getting into a routine, being together on a daily basis. Basically, she said to me, 'Your routine is boring.'"

Nia chimed in, "Yes, I mean, here I was, playing Jane Housewife because I hadn't really established myself and my clientele. So I was trying to figure out what this marriage thing was and how not to lose myself in it. I was sort of sensitive and reactive about the challenges of moving away from my support system, developing a new business and negotiating our different lifestyles. When my business began to take off in Michigan I began to have a whole new set of frustrations."

Digging Beneath the Surface Frustrations for a More Meaningful Connection

Theodore and Nia were typical of many couples we worked with who believed they had many frustrations that all needed to be addressed. We have learned that frustrations are symptoms of a bigger issue of feeling disconnected. Part of our success with this work has been helping couples pinpoint one frustration and then use the MFG process to peel away the layers to determine what needs to be done to restore the feelings of connection - of feeling loved and cared about in a specific way. With practice, couples can use the same steps to apply to other symptoms. Nia and Theodore eventually demonstrated this beautifully.

Melva asked Theodore and Nia to select any one frustration. They consulted each other and then Nina said, "Theodore is always late picking me up at the airport when I travel for work."

Theodore's eyes scanned the ceiling and then returned to Nia, his gaze intent.

Describe the Surface of the Conflict

Melva asked Nia to say more.

"After I've been working and traveling, I want to get home as soon as that airplane lands. When you are not there Theodore, it infuriates me! Like that time I called you before we took off to make sure you knew that we were on time. You said you would be there when I arrived. I called you again before I got my luggage. I was expecting you to be there. But there was no sign of you!" Nia tossed her long locks and sat on the edge of her chair with her back erect. Her voice grew louder.

"45 minutes went by, and I was still sitting and waiting for you, and I couldn't reach you on your cell phone. I was telling myself, 'He's not here. Why isn't he here? Why am I waiting so long? What's the deal here?'" She leaned back in her chair, exasperated. "You know that I don't like waiting for you, particularly around airports. I don't want to be sitting there a minute longer than I have to be. And without fail, when you appear, you don't say a word about why you were late, nor do you apologize."

Theodore had not moved. His eyes were fixed on Nia's face as she swayed back and forth, expressing herself with her body and her hands as she talked.

Dig for the Underlying Feelings

"What additional feelings bubble up for you when you are waiting like that?" Jesse inquired.

"I feel angry. Furious! That's what I feel, Theodore. Furious because you just don't get it." She flung her arms into the air.

"What do you do when you feel furious?" said Melva.

Nia and Theodore had talked about the issue with us before, during our group meeting with all the couples. Nia said that it had taken her a long time to figure out what she did when she was frustrated.

"I'm not proud of it, but I sulk. Oh, yes, I can really sulk. Then I try to get away from him."

"Like withdrawing?" Jesse asked.

"Oh, yes, that's a good way to put it, I withdraw. But before I do, I'll be short with Theodore, or on occasion I might yell at him. But the most dangerous time for us isn't when I'm yelling; it's when I go silent. Going silent is what I traditionally do when I have reached my threshold. When I get to that point I'm out, gone, way back."

What was the Hurt Underneath Your Anger?

"And when you are silent are you aware of what is hurting you?" Melva inquired.

"Yes, *abandoned* and *unattended to*. But tonight I realize I am also feeling *frozen out*. It's a real empty and lonely feeling. That's what hurts the most. What hurts me even more is I really believe that the reason you are late, Theodore, is because you don't feel I'm important enough to you to get there on time."

The Fear Underneath the Hurt

"Stay with those feelings of hurt," Melva said. "Close your eyes and let yourself go to the next layer of feelings. What scares you about the possibility that Theodore's frustrating behavior will continue?"

Nia closed her eyes and took several deep breaths. She was silent for several minutes, and then began to share her feelings of fear. Theodore was giving her his undivided attention.

"I don't like this feeling. It's big for me because being scared brings up a whole lot of issues about how I don't want to depend on another person. That's why I'm so self-sufficient. It scares me that I allow myself to depend on you and then you let me down." Tears flowed from her eyes.

"So when you, Theodore, don't say anything when you show up late, it's more painful than you will ever know. That is why I get so upset. And when I get upset, you just wait for my anger to blow over so you don't have to deal with it. That makes it even more difficult for me because I have a desire to say or do something more and I don't have the opportunity to verbalize it. When we get to that level, my need to avoid mortal combat is greater than my need to fix or address the situation. So I choose not to address it sometimes. Nothing is said, and then I wonder how we can sit there and pretend it didn't happen. How can we ignore it? That doesn't make sense to me."

"I start thinking about how I don't need to be married. I start thinking about what I need most in the moment. And what I know I need most is to be creative. So when Theodore doesn't respond, and we get stuck, there's a reflex part of my mind that says to me, *I could be in another country right about now doing something else. If this doesn't work out, I have options. If I can't feel that he is willing to get along with me, then why am I in this relationship?*"

What Are Your Early Memories of these Same Hurts and Fears?

"Keep your eyes closed," Jesse suggested. "Let's go even deeper and connect the essence of your hurt and fear to your history."

"I absolutely have a connection," Nia said right away. "I have lots of memories of having to sit around waiting for my parents to pick me up. I was always the last kid picked up from whatever. There was never an apology or an acknowledgment like, 'You know, sweetheart, you had to wait because this was what happened.' It was more like, 'Well, I'm the adult in the situation. Tough! Your opinion doesn't matter, and if you wait you wait. So shut up!'"

"I don't remember them being late picking up my sister. She didn't have to wait. It seemed like everybody went out of their way to please her. She didn't have any problem bluntly speaking up for herself. It didn't matter who she was talking to—children or adults—she would tell you whatever was on her mind. When she was blunt, they'd said, 'That's cute.'"

"But that didn't work for me, so I decided to go out of my way to become a Pleaser and make sure everything was okay. It's also about wanting so much to feel heard when someone lets me down, especially my parents. I wanted so much to be heard. Instead of having the opportunity to share what I thought and felt, I was ignored or told what to think and feel. Based on that, I decided that nothing that I said was of value. I think I must have decided that it wasn't worth trying to get my point across over petty stuff. If anyone wants to push my buttons, just keep me from speaking my opinion about things that are important to me"

Nia had put her finger on the childhood memories that were seeping into the present, coloring her already unpleasant experience of having to wait for Theodore.

Find the Gold Nugget: Identify Your Wants and Desires

"So," Melva said, "past meets present. But now you have an opportunity for a healing outcome. So when Theodore is late and doesn't tell you why and doesn't talk about it, if you could have anything you wanted, what would that be?"

Nia and Theodore had witnessed other couples going through the Mining for Gold process, and Nia then asked, "Was this where I am in the candy store and get to ask for anything I want, as big as I want?"

"Yes. This is that time," Melva replied.

"Actually," Nia said, "I thought about this one many times while I was sitting at the airport waiting for Theodore. I don't ever want to wait again, ever in life." She looked at Theodore. "I want you to be so happy that I am coming home that you get there two hours early and greet me at the gate with a dozen roses and then have dinner ready for us when we arrive home."

"Great job!" Melva responded. "If you expressed that desire in more realistic terms, what would you say?"

"I know that one, there is no question about it. The main thing I want is for Theodore to be at the airport when I arrive.

"And, if you are late, what I need from you and what I needed from my parents back then is for you to make room to hear why I am so upset. And if you are late, I want you to always make room to hear all of my anger and to reflect it back, to tell me how it makes sense and that you can imagine how upset I am. And then apologize." Nia had identified the first golden nugget.

Forge the Golden Keys: Ask For What You Want

"Okay, Nia," Melva asked. "Will you make it more specific?"

"Oh, I wrote the three new behaviors, and I refined what I wrote while I was preparing for tonight's session." Nia flipped through her workbook and took out the revised sheet. "My first request for you, Theodore, is for the next 30 days for you to be at the airport and at baggage claim when the plane arrives."

"My second request is for the next 30 days, if you are going to be late, for you to apologize, tell me why you are late, and listen to how it affects me."

"My third request is, for the next 30 days, for you to not only be on time, but to have a hot meal ready for us when we get home so I can relax as soon as possible. That's what I want." She put her sheet down and winked at Theodore.

"All three requests fit the guidelines. They are short, positive, specific, and doable," Jesse confirmed.

Melva watched Theodore as Nia shared her three behavior change requests. She noticed that he appeared to hold his breath somewhat. "Breathe, Theodore," she advised. "You have a chance to let Nia know how easy, hard, or extra hard each behavior request is."

"I know," Theodore said. "I can tell you now, they are all hard. Now that third one is extra hard. It would be enough of a challenge for me to get to the airport on time; but it would be too much to have a meal prepared. I know I have to pick one and I was thinking about this. The one I think I can do is to be at the airport on time."

Unlock and Open the Golden Door: Identify the Payoffs for Each Partner

Theodore had completed a very important step, making a commitment to fulfill Nia's desire to have an easier transition when she got home after traveling. It was now time for both Nia and Theodore to identify the healing and growth payoff for each.

Jesse turned to Nia. "You have already referred to what would heal within you when you stated how important it is to you that Theodore be on time to pick you up at the airport. What is the most significant part of the healing for you?"

Nia said, "Now I realize it was about feeling important to you, Theodore."

Many couples have difficulty getting clear about the healing because they don't naturally think about the internal transformation that can take place if they receive a more positive response from their partner. So Melva asked, "Would any other healing take place for you?"

"Yes, it helps that I have had time to think about it and talk about it with Theodore. I know there is a distinction between my experience with Theodore and with my parents. However, that feeling I have inside about neither one picking me up on time would begin to heal because you, Theodore, will show up for me and hear how it affects me when you don't." Nia was quiet, continuing to think about the healing for her. "Yes, that fits!" she concluded.

"Okay, Theodore," Jesse said. "You will develop a relationship skill when you give Nia this gift. What will it be?"

"What I came up with when we talked about this before was that it would be an opportunity to make you happy, Nia. I now know that this behavior will let you know that you are important to me. I do want to demonstrate that to you. It will help to create balance for me."

"So let's explore this a little more in terms of the specific skill you would be developing," Melva asked. "When we explained in the group session how difficult it was for some people to initiate contact with their partners when they are feeling stressed, would that fit for you? Was that a skill that you might develop?"

"I hadn't thought about it that way, but maybe you are right. It certainly has not worked for me to wait for her anger to blow over. Maybe we can get back to enjoying each other faster if I follow through in the way she asked. That will also help me to make space to hear what is going on with her as well as to be aware of what is going on with me."

"Yes, if you do, you will hit the bull's-eye of what she needs in the moment," Jesse said.

Same Situation, Different Realities: Mining for Gold for Theodore

It was Theodore's turn to explore what was going on under the surface for him when he was late picking up Nia at the airport.

Describe the Surface of the Conflict

"She said I don't get it. *She* is the one who doesn't get it. Nia, the problem is that you are short with me or you ignore me. Can't you see I am *happy* to see you when I get to the airport?"

Theodore's reaction was an excellent example of the same picture with two different and opposite realities, and his process illustrated how difficult it can be for one partner to understand the reality of the other partner and how they get triggered.

Even though Theodore had just completed the healing and growth part of Nia's process, it was important for Nia to understand what was beneath the surface of his frustrating behavior and to learn the bigger picture of his impatience with her.

The process of Mining for Gold teaches us that in order to break this kind of cycle each of us needs to shift away from being frozen in our way of reacting to the other person's frustrating behavior. We need to pay attention to our own feelings and reality and describe our own internal experience, in order to get to the source of our habitual behavior.

Dig for the Underlying Feelings

To start the shifting process, Jesse asked Theodore, "So when Nia is short and impatient with you, sulks, withdraws from, or ignores you, what do you feel inside?"

Not everyone is aware of how to adequately describe their own feelings, so generally we help them to identify sensations in their body that correspond to emotions. Theodore experienced being in a family where he longed for touch, and after attending a weekend workshop and being a member of a group, he had a better understanding of the language of feelings.

He thought about it for a few moments, and then said, "Part of what I felt was anger, that I could not have a discussion about what's on going without it becoming heavily charged."

"Good job!" Melva coached. "Now, what do you *do* when you feel this way?"

"Well," Theodore said, "I get angry."

"Getting angry is what you *feel*," Jesse clarified. "And there is also something you say or do when Nia is upset with you. Can you tell us about that? What is the behavior you do?"

"What do I do? Oh! First I try to get a response when she ignores me."

"How do you do that?" Melva inquired.

"I wait."

"And when that doesn't work?" Jesse asked.

"When that doesn't work I shut down. I become silent and don't respond. I just walk away from the issue, both emotionally and intellectually. Physically I'm there taking the brunt of her anger, and on some level I know that her anger is expressing something that she needs to complete."

Again, we learned from Theodore's experience what happens when we get triggered. In the moment it becomes a matter of emotional survival. So we stay defensive without being aware of what is really going on within us, below the surface of our external behavior.

What Was the Hurt Underneath Your Anger?

Melva said to Theodore, "We want to help you to be in touch with and describe what hurts you beneath the anger, when you get quiet. Take a deep breath and scan your body. What are you aware of?"

Theodore asked for a few minutes and took several breaths. Then he made eye contact with Nia. "Hurt", he said quietly. "It hurts when you withdraw from me, Nia," His voice cracked. "I feel like you don't care for me." He paused, downcast.

Melva asked him to say more about his hurt. Since Nia and Theodore had already worked through this process at the workshop we'd held with all the couples, Jesse prompted him by asking, "What did you learn at the workshop?"

"What I wrote down," Theodore said, "was feelings of neglect, unimportance, being unappreciated, and not being acknowledged."

Jesse asked, "Do those feelings fit this frustration?"

Theodore took another deep breath and acknowledged, "Yes, they fit."

What Was the Fear Below the Hurt?

Melva asked, "What is the fear you wrote down previously, at the workshop?"

"I am glad that I thought about this before. I wrote down other feelings words like, *indifference, disapproval,* and *being taken for granted.*"

Jesse asked, "So what do you imagine would happen to you if Nia continued to ignore, neglect or not appreciate you?"

"I would not have the openness or sharing I have always thought about and need."

What Are Your Early Memories of these Same Hurts and Fears?

"I imagine that you might have a lot of feelings about this," Melva said. "Take a moment and travel back in time to your relationship history, back to your life before Nia. What do these feelings remind you of? We have clues from what you said earlier about your family dynamics. What comes to mind now?"

"A feeling of indifference regarding my opinion and presence comes to my mind. It was like I was being taken for granted by people who were important to me, like my dad."

Theodore was the first born and only son in his family. His parents were the first born in their respective families as well, and as the first born in two generations, there were high expectations that Theodore would go to college.

He also had a younger sister, and had good feelings about his relationship with his mom because she was so open with him that he could share his thoughts and feelings with her throughout his lifetime.

"My Dad played the heavy all the time," Theodore recalled. "I know he cared but I didn't experience it a lot. As a teenager I started to wonder why I wasn't having conversations with him except at the dinner table. It wasn't that he didn't have anything to say; I think he just became a very good listener. Maybe he developed that skill growing up. It probably wasn't all that happy, so he learned to be quiet, and learned to be very caring but not very vocal. I found out many years after my paternal grandfather died that he was basically the same way."

"One significant experience I had with was Dad was him buying me a winter coat. It was one of the proudest days of my life. I loved the coat because he bought if for me. And that was just a great moment for me. But it wasn't a whole lot of conversation and intimacy. That kind of sharing between us just wasn't there. It was kind of *I'm the parent, you're the child. Do what I tell you to do.* He wasn't abusive, just stand-offish."

Until Theodore was in his late 20s, his relationship with his father remained rather formal, he explained. "We talked, but it was not an open exchange. He was the parent. I was the son. To this day it's not as open as it could be, or how I want it to be over the long term. And so we're still working on that. My mother was different. She had no qualms about telling me how she really felt. That was one way she let me know she cared. The other way was that she was always hugging us. I think one of the reasons she was so caring was because she was the oldest of five kids and took on the role of being the second mom to her brothers and sisters."

As for his parents' relationship, Theodore said that he didn't notice a lot of intimacy between them.

"But they got through that and today I can see ways that they show affection. So it's seems strange after me being out of the house over 10 years to come back and see that. But it's good to see the affectionate way that they treat each other. And my dad isn't really physically affectionate and doesn't use touchy-feely words. He will probably never be that way, because it's just not how he is. And because he's not, my mom isn't either, with him. So she understands that when they are in public not to do those kinds of things. But she's different with my sister and myself and other people. With others she is very affectionate. She just doesn't show that with him, because my dad's uncomfortable with it. It's not natural for him, so I think it has helped me to gain an understanding of that."

Find the Gold Nugget: Identify Your Wants and Desires

"We know there was something you needed, both from your parents as well as from Nia," Jesse said. "What was that?"

"I've thought about that for a long time. What I needed was conversation. That would be an acknowledgment that my presence was important and that

I mattered. That it was okay for me to be different in what I felt and did. I spent a lot of years looking for dad's approval. I can see how my actions now at work and home are about seeking approval. I may disguise it a little differently, by asking things like 'Well, what did you think about this? How did this go?' But basically it is a search for approval."

Jesse asked, "So, how would you describe that as a global desire for Nia?"

"That's easy." Turning toward Nia he said, "My global desire is that you, Nia, will never get mad at me when I am late, ever again; and that you ask me about what I am going through every single time."

Nia smiled. "This is my time to be quiet and listen," she said.

"I know I have to be more realistic," said Theodore. "If I were to be realistic, I would say that instead of staying mad and focusing on what I did wrong, that you listen to what I have to say when I explain myself, and then get to a place of understanding and move on."

Forge the Golden Keys: Ask for What You Want

"What would that be like in terms of three new behaviors?" Jesse inquired. "What would you ask Nia for?"

Theodore was ready with his requests. "My first request is that for the next four weeks; when I explain my reasons for being late, that you drop the issue and move forward, move on, meaning just let it go."

"My second request is, for the next 30 days, when you get angry, instead of shutting down and holding what I did over my head for a long period of time, for us to talk and discuss the situation until we both understand through a process of dialogue."

"My third request is, for the next 30 days, when you are not ready to talk, to postpone it but then be ready within 24 hours. And when you're ready, you bring it up."

Nia listened to each request and repeated them, then ranked each one. "Well, the first one is hard; the second one is easier. The third request is easy, too."

She chose one change of behavior – number two – and offered it as her gift to Theodore.

Unlock and Open the Golden Door: Identify the Positive Payoffs for Each Partner

"Just a reminder about our next step," Melva mentioned. "This is the part where you tell Nia how her gift of the new behavior will affect you in a healing way. Theodore, what do you believe will begin to heal within you when Nia gives you this gift of initiating a dialogue about your frustration and hers until you both understand?

Theodore thumbed through his notes to find his worksheet.

"I wrote that receiving this gift would allow me to feel closer to her the way I wanted to feel closer to my dad, and the way I felt with my mom. I would also get closure and focus on the good things we have, instead of worry and feeling angry, neglected, and rejected."

He looked up and added, "Now that we have been talking about what happened with my family, I would add to this list the gift of feeling that my presence is important and that I matter. I do need to know that I matter to you, Nia."

Nia tossed her flowing locks and said, "You do matter to me, Honey. I just need you to come through for me in very specific ways. And I know I have a job to do also. I have some stretching to do for you, as well."

Nia then shared how this change of interaction would help her grow. "The relationship skill this will help me to develop is the ability to put clear, intelligible words to my emotions when I am upset with you, Theodore. I will also develop deeper intimacy with you through being vulnerable instead of just taking care of myself. I will depend on myself and become more of the person I dreamed I wanted to be when I listened to those love songs back when I was growing up."

The Importance of Healing and Growth in Relationships

We know from personal and professional experience that consistently implementing new behaviors in relationships can be difficult because it involves entering unexplored territory. But as we heal the pain of current relationships, we also heal what was experienced in our relationship histories of the past.

Growth takes place when each partner provides the caring words, behaviors and touch desired by their partner. These behaviors lead to feeling loved in a very specific way. The degree to which a person feels loved can also have an impact on how loveable they feel. The degree to which a person feels loveable can have an impact on how loving they are motivated to be, so the cycle is a synergistic one.

An internal healing and transformation occurs when partners receive what they have longed for. When they consistently receive what they have always wanted, a healing occurs both in their present as well as past life history. By identifying the growth that can occur as a result of consistently following through with behaviors requested by a partner and then practicing those behaviors, relationship skills that have been underdeveloped are also likely to develop.

In the case of Theodore and Nia, the surface issue for her was not being picked up at the airport on time. As she explored beneath the surface, she was reminded of all the times in her childhood when her parents were always late picking her up. Theodore could imagine her as a child waiting for her parents. He could understand how she might have felt and could have greater empathy and compassion for her. Then he could make the connection about how she was likely to feel when he was late picking her up. So when Theodore choose to give her his gift of picking her up on time at the airport, Nia felt important to him, valued, loved, and cared for.

Theodore's desire was for them to find more productive ways of addressing conflicts. This was healing for him because he could start to have the intimate talks he yearned for with his parents as a child.

He felt that his presence was important and that he mattered to Nia. This enabled both of them to understand the bigger issue instead of reacting with anger, shutting down, and becoming entrenched in conflict for long periods of time.

Each time Theodore followed through by picking Nia up on time at the airport, he shifted from self-absorption to focus on the "we," an important relationship skill. His behavior demonstrated to Nia that she was important to him and that she could trust him to be there for her when she needed him. This helped him also, by encouraging him to be responsible for – and responsive to – Nia.

And while Theodore may have done 100 other things to communicate his love and caring for her, many of those "other things" were less important to her than was the specific act of picking her up on time. He did not have to guess what she might want or need. She had communicated her request to him in a way that he understood. He knew exactly what she wanted and the "behavior" that he needed to demonstrate. Each time he followed through he "hit the bull's eye" of fulfilling her needs in the moment.

Theodore felt better about himself as a man and a partner when he perceived that he was succeeding at making Nia happy, a goal that was very important to him.

"It certainly had not worked for me to wait for Nia's anger to blow over. But after understanding the whole process, I knew that we could get back to enjoying each other faster when I followed through and was there for her in the way she had asked."

The growth for Nia was expressed as an increased ability to put her emotions into clear, intelligible words when she was upset with Theodore. She didn't have to relive those awful arguments she witnessed with her parents. She could successfully communicate her hurts and desires to him, without raging and becoming emotionally distant.

The Mining for Gold process gave her the tools she needed to communicate with Theodore in a way that ensured that he was better able to hear her and then respond in a positive way.

The Importance of Healing and Growth in Relationships

The MFG process illustrates (through Theodore's gift of understanding Nia's frustration) the power of *hearing* the deeper meaning beneath our partner's frustration. Theodore can finally comprehend the bigger picture for Nia at an emotional, feeling level. We call this "feeling level" empathy and compassion.

The behavior change he chose to give Nia as a gift provided a healing outcome for Nia, a response she had longed for her entire lifetime. As Theodore followed through by picking Nia up on time at the airport, he showed that she was important to him and that she could trust him to be there for her when she needed him. The growth for him as a man, as well as a husband, expanded and brought out positive and attractive character traits already within him.

Theodore really wanted to make Nia happy and by following the "Platinum Rule" – do unto others as they would *like to be done unto* – he was effective and more competent as a husband.

Nia also showed the power of her gift to Theodore and how it supported her growth as a woman and a wife. By approaching and addressing her frustration with him in a more productive way, she allowed Theodore to be healed. He began to feel that his presence was important and that he mattered to her, which was tantamount to feeling closer to her.

While each partner approached the conflict differently, both were empowered by their internal commitments to change. By not exhibiting reactive behaviors that simply added more fuel to the conflict without dealing with deeper and more fundamental dynamics, they experienced real intimacy and healing growth.

Nia demonstrated that sometimes the difficulty in getting unstuck from frustrations when we are upset with our partners is that we lack the specific skills necessary to let us put our emotions into clear, intelligible words.

This process assisted her in communicating her hurts and desires beneath the surface of her internalized intense anger, before she shut down or distanced herself from Theodore emotionally. This allowed Theodore to hear her and respond to her in a positive way, which was a payoff for both of them.

An Update: Where They Are Now

A year later we saw Theodore and Nia at a group session and Theodore was ready to give us an update.

"I am very clear that no one else matters to me when it comes to the grand scheme the way Nia does. She means a great deal to me, and because she does, the stakes are very high. I know I can live without her, but I don't want to. I have decided that I wanted to be more communicative with Nia and our family than my father was with my siblings and me. So I'll work hard to make sure I do my part."

Nia said, "One of the greatest things about our marriage and the intimacy that we have achieved is that I feel it's okay to put anything out there and Theodore will accept it as something to deal with. And he certainly knows he can tell me things.   This Mining for Gold process had taught me to understand the difference between a statement of expectations and a statement of request when we hit a communication bump."

"I know I spend a lot of my time having my own little fantasy of what I might say and what he could say back. But I've learned the difference between realistic and unrealistic expectations. If there's something I want from him, I now know how to state that fully and clearly."

"For me, when something happens and we don't deal with it, I feel like I'm getting better at saying, 'I recognize that something just happened because I'm feeling this feeling.' When I get this feeling, I know that I am two seconds away from going into either yelling or silence. I want to highlight it, and I want us to do whatever we can to address it."

"So I think that while Theodore is getting better at verbalizing, I still have to prompt him. I've learned to recognize that if I let it go that he might minimize things and then I'll pay for it later. I think I am increasing my skill for recognizing that we are in a moment, and calling upon that skill to at least mark that moment and acknowledge it verbally so we can talk about it. So we're getting closer. I stand by what he said about us mattering to each other."

"I continue to notice that when I get so emotional what is happening is more about me not being able to put my feelings into understandable language. Not knowing what to say to clearly mark the moment, without it coming out so nonlinear and dramatic and hard to understand. For me, it has been about finding ways to address Theodore's frustrating behavior in language that is understandable. Or at least to be able to say something is going on. And that I don't have words for it yet but we need to come back to it."

"And he is getting much better at describing what is going on with him. He's a thinking person; I'm a feeling person. His thinking doesn't work when I'm feeling and I don't want to talk about it. There have been times when we've been at it for, like, two hours. I'm so grateful for the village of other mothers and my close friends that I have now, where I have an extended opportunity to express myself. It's good practice to prepare my words for Theodore"

Theodore added, "I think the other growth opportunity for me is to express myself more in a manner that Nia can hear. I have gotten better at listening, too. I let her respond, 'cause sometimes it just takes her a long time to bring it out. On occasion, I've been really stiff. I think I'm embarrassed about it. It's probably an issue of control. I'm looking to be in control of a situation. So, to just let go and allow myself to be in someone else's arms without a care in the world isn't something that I do very comfortably. And that's something that I'm working to improve or at least soften. I think about what my father would do. Usually he would be there physically, but he would be zoned out somewhere else. Like my dad, I learned to withdraw. I'm present, but I'm not present. I'm physically there, but I go into my invincible, silent mode because if I didn't, I might attack."

"We've come to a point where we're actually wanting to talk. Instead of just stopping at a point, now she'll talk about and explain her feelings instead of doing what she used to do. When we first came together, she would just get mad and wouldn't explain why. For me, it just didn't make any sense. We can talk about it now. We can come to a place of mutual understanding. We can tell each other what hurts and what we need from each other.

"I may not always agree with Nia," he said, "but I do have to understand her. I've learned not to commit to anything I'm not willing to do. And I think I surprise her when I say, 'Well, no, I can't do that because I don't necessarily agree.'"

"She gets upset with me not because I'm wrong about something, but because I don't try to understand what she's saying. So, I'm learning to talk more. I'm letting her know more about what I'm thinking. I still internalize a great deal, but at least I'm starting to work through that and share my thoughts with her."

Nia continued, "I told my mother that I was having a really good time being together with Theodore. A year ago this conversation would have been really difficult to have. Now we can really talk about our hopes, dreams, and desires—about finding that place inside of us that keeps us connected."

Theodore looked at Nia and said, "We've found the balance."

They embraced and kissed. All around the room we noticed the smiling faces and sparkling eyes of others in the group celebrating.

A further update. Three years later, Theodore and Nia became parents of a beautiful bouncing baby boy.

CHAPTER 9
JOSH AND JEAN'S STORY
IT'S NEVER TOO LATE TO FIND LOVE

"Getting Better At Understanding – And Being Understood"

This couple reminded us that love can be found at any age, and that we should never give up on the love we desire with that one special person. These two found each other later in life and were grateful for their life together. They were a couple of mixed heritage; Josh was Jewish and in his seventies; Jean was in her sixties and was raised as an Episcopalian. They had been married for 15 years, and this was the second marriage for both. As grandparents, they had five adult married children from previous marriages.

Of the two, Jean was the more verbal and outgoing. When we first met her, she greeted us with an open, gentle smile and a warm, inviting voice. She made instant eye contact – with her bright blue eyes – and gave us the feeling of acceptance and a genuine desire to know us better. Extremely talented in a number of areas, Jean was retired from university public relations and fund-raising. She remained an artist, a trained vocalist and pianist, a stock market wizard, and a gourmet cook.

Josh, at 76, enjoyed an exceptional intellect and was gifted in a number of areas. A retired physician, he was a computer genius, mathematician, and an engineer. He especially enjoyed challenging his mind by playing computer games and repairing old clocks.

When we first met him, Josh appeared somewhat distracted and detached. He made eye contact initially, and then glanced away while we talked to him. It seems he wasn't paying attention – that is, until he began to reiterate what we'd said, word for word. Josh was a generous man who would give you the shirt off his back.

Jean said, "I think I really fell head over heels in love with Josh a few months after we met. I was very attracted to him, and he had decided to forego the '19-year-old tootsie pies' and get serious about a real woman. So he was turning on all of his charm, giving it everything he had, and was calling me constantly."

"It was such a breath of fresh air," she went on, "to talk to someone who wanted to talk and share something of himself." I was so enchanted. I had spent three years as a divorced woman and thought those passionate feelings were all in my past. But let me tell you, my hormones started raging in overdrive. In a way, it was a little unnerving and tough. It took me a while to trust his generosity of spirit and his wanting to be with me – to trust what I was experiencing."

"We talked and talked," Josh added, "She helped me with my self-doubts and our feelings for each other just sort of grew on us. Once I caught on, we got married right away. Remember, in your later years of life, you just don't have a lot of time to mess around."

From Romance to Frustration

After Josh and Jean got together, it didn't take long for them to grow aware of little behavioral annoyances that pushed their respective buttons. Jean was quite clear when she said, "You can love somebody to death and still fight with them."

"We loved each other," Josh added, "but still had problems we had to work out."

Said Jean, "For me, a lot of the disputes we had early in our marriage were about who was in charge. We struggled with that for a long time. As newly-weds, our first frustration was that my daughter was living with us, for the first three years of our marriage."

Jean's daughter was attending law school. "She had her law books all over the house," Josh said, "Twenty-four hundred square feet of law books. And when she was studying, she couldn't stand any noise. She expected everyone in the house to respect her need for absolute quiet. Then when she went to sleep, she still wanted quiet. I was playing a video game, and she said *He's way too noisy*. She was like the princess, and I was the pea."

Jean agreed, "She *was* a princess."

"You don't have to be Jewish to be a princess," Josh pointed out. "She had three years of law school, and we started counting the minutes until she would go."

"Well, she graduated from law school," Jean continued. "She married and moved away."

But the problem did not go away. "Then," Josh explained, "the problem was that Jean spent so much time talking to her daughter on the telephone. I had a hard time with that, but didn't say much."

He added that when Jean's talking to her daughter started bothering him, he elected not to talk about it. "I got absorbed in my computer games. I just sort of said, 'Well, I have to accept this other person for the way she is and make the best of it.'" He chose his battles carefully. "If I'm going to fight for something, it's got to be something worth it. I don't believe in bickering."

"I'll tell you what I would fight for," Jean declared. "I would fight for a mother's right to support her child. Josh, you don't understand how much she needs me when she calls. I don't know how to get through to you about this."

Melva stopped them and explained that their present conversation was about a very important past issue. The problem was that they were approaching it only on the surface.

The good news was that another way was possible. Instead of skimming the surface, where their frustrations separated them, they could go beneath and explore the hurts and fears being triggered by their current conflict. Jean and Josh were up to the challenge and they chose to do the Mining for Gold Process together.

Josh had put his finger on the frustration that he wanted to address in the Mining for Gold process. Jean was behaving in a way that really pushed his buttons. His job was to figure out why her actions bothered him so much.

For her part, Jean needed to grow more aware of how she was affecting Josh, because the impact of her actions on him constituted her blind spot.

Digging beneath Surface Frustrations for a More Meaningful Connection

Describe the Surface of the Conflict

Josh began the process by describing Jean's frustrating behavior. It took a while for him to put her frustrating behavior into a single sentence.

"Jean, it is frustrating when you spend more time on the phone talking to your daughter than attending to me."

Jesse asked him, "What else do you feel when she frustrates you this way?"

"I get angry."

"And when you feel angry with Jean about this, how do you behave?"

"Oh!" he said, looking at Jean.

"Josh," she said, "you know what you do."

"Well, I play my computer games."

Then he thought a little more about it and said, "Okay, I sulk. Was that what you wanted me to say?"

"It is what you do," Jean said. "And if I interrupt you when you're angry at me, you get a little abrupt. If I tell you that dinner is ready you don't say anything at first. Then when I tell you again, you flare up and snap at me and say, 'I heard you!' Isn't that what happens?"

Josh didn't answer at first. He looked down at the floor.

"That's not the only thing you do," Jean added.

Again Josh looked away, then turned back to her, shifting in his chair. "I know. I know," he said briskly. "I tell you 'no' when you ask me to do something."

His reaction to her in front of us helped to further illustrate what he did whenever he felt disconnected from Jean. Sulking, being abrupt, flaring up, and saying "no" were his ways of showing that he felt a loss of connection with her. To learn more about how to restore that connection, Josh needed to dig underneath the surface and find his deeper reactions.

Dig for the Underlying Feelings

Few couples understand that at the core of most conflicts between them is a feeling of disconnection. Losing a sense of connection is always painful. But generally this pain is expressed through argument, withdrawal, criticism, or raising one's voice, instead of by accurately identifying the hurt feelings and then expressing them.

Josh knew he felt frustrated and angry. But because he wasn't accustomed to being aware of his hurt and communicating it, he needed support to explore this feeling.

Melva asked him, "What is the hurt below your anger?"

After thinking for a minute, Josh looked up at Jean and then lowered his head. A tear rolled down his cheek, and he said, "Jean just doesn't understand."

"Just doesn't understand what?" Jean sat straight up in her chair, irritation in her voice. "Don't you understand how much my daughter means to me? Can't you see that she needs my support? She's my *daughter*, Josh."

Jesse asked Jean if she'd be willing to learn more about what Josh was trying to teach her about his internal reality. Melva explained that what he was experiencing internally wasn't the same thing that she was reacting to. They each had an entirely different view of the reality of what they were talking about.

Josh looked up again and began to share his thoughts with Jean. She was about to interrupt him, but Melva asked that she first give him a chance to offer more information.

"Go ahead, Josh," Jesse told him. "Jean needs to hear what happens inside you when she spends so much time talking with her daughter on the phone. Tell her what you feel. She wants to know, and she needs to know. This isn't about right and wrong; this is about two different experiences and two different needs."

Josh was looking directly at Jean, his breathing faster and deeper. She sat back in her chair. He gazed at her for about two minutes more, then responded, "When Jean spends so much time talking to her daughter, I feel excluded, like I'm not important or cared about. I feel like she doesn't understand or care about what's going on with me."

What Fear Underlies Your Hurt?

Josh had become aware of his hurt and articulated it. Next, he needed to get in touch with his fear that something he wanted or needed would not get fulfilled. He'd probably need a little help shifting from the hurt to the fear, so we slowed down to give Josh more time to experience his hurt feeling more fully, knowing that exploring those feelings was new for him.

When he began to tremble slightly, Melva asked about his fear. In an almost inaudible tone he told us, "I'm frightened that I won't get the response I want and need from Jean."

He was in tears. Jesse asked what else he was afraid of. Still in an almost inaudible voice, he said, "I feel incompetent to get what I need from Jean." He turned to his wife. "Jean," he said, "you can't imagine what it's like for me. It scares me that I might not be able to handle this much hurt. What scares me most is feeling criticized for hurting. This is how I feel you control me. This is a vulnerable spot for me."

What Are Your Earliest Memories of Similar Hurts and Fears?

Now that Josh had recognized his hurt and fear, he was ready to identify memories of similar ones earlier in his life. Often this leads people into talking about what we call their *core wound*— a very old, painful feeling left over from childhood.

Melva asked Josh what old feeling his frustration reminded him of. Josh had been in counseling before, so he had some insight into the importance of making a connection between past and present. However, at first he couldn't think of a connection because he was so absorbed in the pain of the here and now. This was not unusual. He said he needed more time to think about it, because as far as he knew, the feelings applied only to this situation with Jean. Jesse encouraged him to give himself more time, and he did, returning to the process after first attending a session of individual therapy.

When Josh returned, he said he thought he was ready to make a connection between how he felt about Jean spending so much time with her daughter and how he felt growing up in his family. In a sad voice, tears steaming down his face, he said, "These feelings remind me of something old, something I never really investigated. The painful times I had growing up with my parents. I don't like to think about it, because it hurts so much. I spent years trying to push these feelings down.

"I ache inside when I think about this, but I now know what the connection is. When Jean spends so much time on the phone with her daughter, I'm waiting for *my* time. When she finally hangs up, and I tell her how I feel, she gets angry with me. When that happens, it feels like the story of my life—not being loved or cared about.

It's about waiting for someone I love to make time for me. When I was growing up, my mother didn't make enough time for me. I felt she didn't care about me. My father did spend some time with me, but those were mostly painful times. Most of our time together was him telling me what to do. He controlled me. I tried to please him, but wasn't successful. If I didn't do what he said, the way he said, he would criticize me. I just wanted him to love me.

"It's hard for me to say this." He paused. Jean's face softened, and she reached over to touch his arm. Josh continued. "I grew up feeling so frustrated and hurt by my father criticizing and controlling me. He never said he loved me or cared about me, didn't tell me about the good things I did. It was like I couldn't do anything right. All I wanted was his approval. When he said hurtful things to me, so many I can't recall them all, my mother kept silent. It seemed as if she became invisible. I remember once saying to myself that I needed a mother. I felt that so many times, I know. She just didn't show any interest in me.

"As an adult, I sat in an analyst's chair for five years and never once mentioned my mother. I don't know why; maybe I didn't want to be disloyal to her. Even now I feel somewhat guilty saying anything negative about her because she was a lovely woman. Other people experienced her completely differently than I did. It was so hard to describe how painful that was."

As Josh recalled painful memories, Jean was touched by his words and began to cry. She stood up, walked over to his chair, and sat on his lap. Then she hugged him tightly and said, "I had no idea that talking to my daughter brought up so much pain for you. I'm so sorry." They began to weep together.

A few minutes later, Josh said, "Now I understand how the past shows up in the present. How can this be happening again? I thought I never had to deal with this again! I know Jean loves and cares about me, but I haven't been able to understand why my frustration with her hurts so much. You know, when her daughter was living with us, I was tremendously jealous of her. And to this day, I fret when Jean talks to her a long time on the phone while I'm waiting for her to talk to me. I know it goes way back into my childhood."

Jesse asked Josh what feeling surfaced for him. "Was it fear that her daughter would take Jean away from you? Fear that she'd take time away from you? Or fear of abandonment?"

Josh replied, "I guess I was feeling my mother not caring about me and not loving me enough, all over again. But this is the first time I've been able to voice it and accept it for what it is. Of course I love Jean's daughter. She's a darling."

Jean replied, "It must have really been difficult, those days when I got mad and told you, 'I'm not your mother.'"

With his new awareness of why he got triggered when Jean spent time talking to her daughter, Josh had completed the first two steps of the Mining for Gold process.

Identify Your Wants and Desires

It was time for Josh to identify the gold Nugget at the core of his issue with Jean. What hidden insights could he use to create a more loving connection with Jean?

The gold Nuggets are the things we *want* from—and with—our partners. They are shaped by our past: What we needed but didn't get from our family, and therefore continue to hunger for in current relationships.

Melva asked Josh what he needed from his mother that she didn't give him, and what he now needed from Jean.

"What I needed was for her to spend enough time with me to show that she was interested in me. Then I'd have felt important, cared about, and supported by my parents. I need you, Jean, to express the same degree of love, importance, and caring to me as you do to your daughter, so you show that you have time and energy for me as well."

Josh added that what he longed for from his father was for him to acknowledge and show interest in what Josh wanted and to help him accomplish it. Jesse asked him to couch his desires in global terms. What would be the most outrageous way of expressing what he wanted?

Josh lowered his head and went into his usual contemplative posture, propping his chin between clasped fingers. We sat patiently while he considered the question and prepared a reply. Thinking in those terms was new territory for Josh, and he asked for a suggestion.

Melva responded, "It would be something like, 'I want you to show me how important I am to you and how much you love me, *before* you talk to your daughter, the *entire time* you talk to your daughter, and *after* you talk to her.'"

"That's global?" Josh asked in surprise. "I think I really do want that, for real."

"Good! Now say that in your own words."

With a big smile, Josh said, "Okay, I got it! My global desire is for you to make me feel important, 100 percent of the time."

Then Jesse asked Josh to put his global desire into more realistic terms.

"Okay, I'll be more practical. My more realistic desire is for you to give me more attention, by setting boundaries with the amount of time you give to your daughter."

Josh's golden nugget was to feel important to Jean and to feel cared about and supported by her—all of which were feelings he had missed during childhood.

Ask for What You Want

It was time for Josh to ask Jean to fulfill his desire in very specific ways to experience a more loving connection with her.

The golden keys are the actual behavioral changes that our partners give us as a gift to fulfill our desires. It's what we get when we forge the nugget of desire into something practical—keys that can open the golden door of intimacy and closeness with our partners.

What is most important about this step is that it provides an opportunity for our partners to develop specific relationship skills. The behavior change requests provide a template for this development to occur.

Josh asked Jean to show him in three specific ways that he was just as important, cared about, and loved as her daughter. By doing so he invited her to grow – an invitation she could either accept or reject. It is our experience that when partners know the positive impact that healing behavior can have on their mates, they are generally motivated to stretch and grow to fulfill their partner's desires as a declaration of love.

Melva asked, "What are three things you'd like Jean to say or do to help you feel important, loved and cared about —even when she spends time talking to her daughter?"

"You see," added Jesse, "it doesn't have to be either-or. It can be both-and."

"Both-and?" asked Josh. "I hadn't thought about it that way. I don't have a clue. I need time to think about this! I'll have more ideas next week."

We agreed, and the following week Josh returned, prepared. "I figured it out," he said, with a serious expression on his face. "This wasn't easy, but I think I came up with something that fits your guidelines, Melva and Jesse."

"Great!" Jesse said. "When you're ready, we're ready to hear what you came up with."

"I'm ready now," Josh replied. He then shared his three requests. His first was that for the next two weeks that Jean limit calls to her daughter to one per day. His second was that for the next 30 days that Jean cut down on the amount of money she spent on gifts for her daughter, and he wanted the two of them to agree on an acceptable amount. His third request was that for the next 30 days when he and Jean were spending time together and her daughter called, Jean would tell her, "I'll call you back."

The next step was for Jean to rank each behavior change request. Jean instantly said that they'd all be hard because each required a significant degree of stretching for her.

We gave her a week to think about it, and at our next session, Jean said she was still trying to figure out the "both/and" idea. Having time with her daughter was so important, and she wanted Josh to understand that. Josh assured her he did and said that the discussion was also about her understanding him.

After we talked a while, Jean said she thought she had it figured out. She turned to Josh and said "As a gift to you I choose number two—spending less of our money on my daughter."

Identify Positive Payoffs for each Partner

Now Josh and Jean were ready to identify the healing and growth that would occur when Jean granted Josh her gift.

"I know what'll begin to heal within me," he said, after giving it some thought.

"Tell Jean," Melva encouraged.

"Okay. Jean, the healing for me when I receive the gift will be feeling more wanted by and connected to you." He became tearful. Jean reached over and hugged him. "I'm not finished," he said. "When you follow through, your behavior will also help heal my childhood wound of not feeling important to my parents, not feeling wanted by my mother, and not feeling my father's approval." Tears began running down his cheeks, and as he finished speaking, he started to sob.

By granting Josh this behavioral gift, Jean also benefited. She stretched into setting boundaries with her daughter—something that Jean admitted was hard for her to do.

Granting Josh this new behavior as a gift was how Jean would grow through the exchange—and how Josh could begin to heal his current and old wounds. The more Jean granted her gift, the more she would grow and strengthen her own ability to be available to her daughter and to Josh, as well as to herself. She would develop deeper trust in her ability to take care of herself and the people that she loved. Jean's daughter and Josh would also be able to connect more deeply with each other.

The golden door was now partially open for them to deepen their connection. But only one half of the blueprint for Jean and Josh to get unstuck was complete. In short, they had more work to do.

Same Situation, Two Different Experiences: Jean's Reality

Jean had a different frustration and internal experience. The places in her that needed healing were likely to compliment, but not be identical to, those that existed within Josh.

Josh's reaction to the relationship between Jean and her daughter was frustrating to Jean. She said that his tendency to sulk, become abrupt, or instantly respond to her requests for help with an emphatic "no," pushed her buttons.

"I react that way," Josh interrupted, "because you're so busy with your daughter that you forget that I'm waiting to spend time with you." But at least for the moment, he missed the point. He couldn't understand how his reactions to Jean were affecting her; their impact on Jean was his blind spot. We needed to explore this frustrating aspect of his behavior.

Describe the Surface of the Conflict

Melva reminded Jean that the dynamic on the surface of any conflict was one partner's counter reaction to the other's reactionary and frustrating behavior. We wanted to make sure she used the MFG format to express her frustration in a manner Josh could hear.

"When you sulk about the amount of time I spend with my daughter," she told him, "I feel irritated. At that moment, the image I have of you is of a spoiled child. This angers me. I would describe my anger as somewhere between pissed-off and enraged. I react by yelling a lot and letting you have a piece of my mind. I march out of the room, but then I realize I haven't gotten everything off my chest, so I march back in and gave you another piece of my mind. I figure you don't know I really mean it until I've said it loudly, at least three times."

She mentioned another of her coping strategies: "The other thing I do is go shopping. I shop until I feel better. If I have enough packages I go out to the car, put them in the trunk, and ask myself, 'Do I feel better?' If not, I go back in the store and buy some more.

"Sometimes, no matter what you say, it just makes things worse. You try all the good techniques, but none of them works because hostility has reached such a pitch. No real communication is going on. Verdicts are being issued, judgments are being pronounced. So at times, it's better to just plain vote with your feet and walk away. That doesn't build closeness, but it does help me to achieve peace and harmony by disengaging from the conflict.

"Inside myself I think that if you want to yell back at me I'm not going to give you an audience. If you want to blame me, you can talk to the wall. I'm out of there. I'm not going to deal with it. Does it build closeness? No. Does it make me happy?

Yes. Why? It's because I don't have to stand there and take what feels like abuse to me. I go and do something that does genuinely make me happy, even though the feeling does not last very long.

"The time-out helps," Jean said, "because my anger dissipates, and then I can come back and talk in a non-hostile way. When I feel intense resentment, I get a tone in my voice and I think I hear my mother talking. I don't like to sound that way. When I become conscious that I'm sounding that way, I split, 'cause I don't want to say anything I'll regret."

Jean had given us a complete picture of her counter reactions and her coping mechanisms. Now it was time for her to look underneath those reactions to discover what might be really going on within herself.

Dig for the Underlying Feelings

When Jesse asked about the hurt that lay below her reactions, she echoed something similar to what Josh had said before:

"I'm not hurt, I'm just pissed."

Melva reminded her that feeling pissed was simply at the surface of what she was feeling. As we talked about this, Jean seemed very much in touch with her anger, so we shifted gears and for about 15 minutes, Jesse took her through a guided meditation to help her get in touch with the hurt.

We noticed a tear rolling down her cheek. Upon completion of the guided meditation, Melva again asked her about the hurt beneath her frustration. Slowly, Jean looked up at Josh.

"I wasn't aware that I was feeling hurt," she said. "During that meditation, what I got in touch with was that the attention I give you isn't good enough. That's what hurts."

To identify the underlying fear we needed to probe deeper.

"I might need another guided imagery," she suggested. We took her through a shorter one, and in about five minutes, she had a response.

"Okay," she said, "I got it. What scares me is that what I give to him will never be enough."

What are Your Memories of Similar Hurts and Fears?

"Jean," Melva said, "We suspect you have felt these feelings of hurt and fear before you met Josh."

"Oh, I know these feelings have a history. I thought I had worked through them, though."

Jean's quivering tone of voice changed to anger. "You know, this is so much like when I was growing up, like all the times I took care of my mother and my brother, and it was never sufficient. My mother was depressed, and my brother was handicapped. I had to take care of them both. That was how I spent most of my time. I was constantly working. There was no time for me. I could never do enough to please anyone in my family." She began to sob.

Josh turned to her. "Jean, honey, I didn't know. I remember you talking about this. When I first heard you say it, I got angry. I was thinking to myself, 'Well, if you feel this way, why do you need me in your life?' But I didn't realize that you were feeling the same way with me.

"Then, as you were talking, I thought about it more and became angry with myself and was telling myself, 'I shouldn't do this. I thought 'how could I do this to her?' I don't want to hurt you, Jean. I love you."

Jesse asked Josh to take a deep breath and keep listening. It was important for him to hear Jean out. It might be difficult, but it was worth it to stay with the process.

But Josh said, "I can't do that right now." So we reminded him what Jean had just learned about him and what he would now be learning about her as a result of just listening and letting her explain. He got quiet for several minutes, and then said, "Okay, I know that's true. But I can't do this right now."

Since we were in the process of supporting Josh to be a safe container for Jean, Jesse took a moment to invite him to go into a safe place inside himself.

This angered Jean because it was her time, but she agreed to wait a few moments for Josh to shift gears and become more attentive so that she would experience a different outcome.

Identify your Wants and Desires

Jean was relieved when Josh told us he was ready to take the next step.

In a soft voice she said slowly, "I really needed and wanted somebody to take care of me. Why couldn't I be taken care of sometimes?" She said what she needed but wasn't getting from Josh was for him to sometimes take care of her by giving her space to bond with her daughter without comment.

It was time for her to express a global desire and she knew immediately what it was. "My global desire is for Josh to never again complain about how I bond with my daughter."

When Jesse asked her to make that global desire more realistic and current, she said, "I want for Josh to understand the bond of a mother and child and why I am giving so much of myself to her."

Ask for What You Want

Jean had some difficulty putting her desire into three positive and practical requests for actions that Josh could take to show her he understood her situation, so we gave her that task as homework. The following week, she returned with her list of three behaviors.

"Wow!" she said. "This was hard, but here's what I came up with." She read them one by one and asked Josh to repeat them.

"My first request, " she said, smiling, "is for you, Josh, to make an appointment to dialogue with me and validate and empathize with me about my daughter's being depressed and her need for her mother's comfort." Josh repeated her request with a grimace. Jean waited until she thought he was ready.

"My second request is for you to validate and emphasize that my daughter is turning to me for support as a way of coping with her problems. You don't have to *agree*. I just want to know that you understand."

Before repeating this request, Josh let out a big sigh. Jean waited to give her third request.

"Okay, Josh. I want you to ask yourself how you can help me support my daughter to get through the tough times, instead of reacting with demands and jealousy. And I am asking for all three of my requests within a 30-day time period."

It was time to rank each of her requests. Josh didn't hesitate to rank Jean's first request as hard. "I've had so much experience with Jean's daughter taking control when she was living with us. For me, it would be like giving her control again. I sighed when you read your second request, because your daughter seems to take care of her problems pretty well in other areas, so I rank this one as hard too."

Before Jean could answer, Josh continued. "You know what else? Your third request was also hard, because I think your daughter is manipulating you."

Melva acknowledged that all the requests were hard for Josh, and reminded him that he had to choose one. Any one that he chose would have a healing affect on Jean, and help him develop a very important relationship skill.

"Isn't there a better way?" Josh asked.

Jesse replied, "There might be, but this is the most effective one we know."

Melva asked if he was willing to try this and see what happened. We wanted him to know that a new, positive experience was available for both him and Jean.

Josh thought for a few moments. "If I have to choose one of the three, I'd choose number two—validating and empathizing that Jean's daughter is turning to her for support. I'll try to understand that, even though it's difficult." Then he added, "This is going to be quite a stretch for me, but I'm willing."

Identify the Positive Payoffs for Each Partner

The next step was for them to identify the healing for Jean and the stretching and growth for Josh.

She seemed excited and told Josh, "You have no idea what this means to me! This is quite a gift. Oh, boy! Let me think about this for a moment. Oh, I know that when you do this for me, I'll feel valuable because someone I love is standing up for me. Yes, that's what it is. When you stand up for me, then I won't feel invisible and unsupported." Jean was grinning. Jesse reminded her that they each had more work to do.

Josh would be developing a relationship skill. "What would that be?" Melva asked.

"I have to think. Let me see," Josh pondered. "My first thought is that I'm growing in my ability to change my negative image of your daughter into a kinder image—seeing her as a child who's struggling and needing support. That would help me become more tolerant."

What did this couple teach us about identifying hurts? We believe that when your partner doesn't give you the love and caring you need, you experience psychological hurt and a sensation of fear.

For Josh, the psychological hurt was feeling criticized, excluded, unimportant, unloved, uncared for, and abandoned whenever Jean spent so much time talking with her daughter on the phone. Digging deeper, he was able to make the connection between the pain he experienced with Jean and the pain he was reliving from the past when his parents used to react to him in a similar way.

When Jean selected the gift of spending less of their money on her daughter, Josh became aware of a very specific, positive impact for him. To him, her gift was a behavioral statement of real value. Feeling *included* was his healing balm.

Jean's hurt wasn't apparent at first, because her anger was in the forefront. She reminded us how anger can be a cover and a defense for avoiding the internal pain of feeling hurt. She even said, "I'm not hurt, I am just pissed." But she wasn't in touch with just how hurt she felt. Once she was able to identify this, Josh could see her in a new light.

Jean didn't have to choose between Josh and her daughter. Her new response was more of a "both/and", rather than an "either/or" position.

Difficult as it was for Josh to validate and empathize with Jean's need to provide support to her daughter, the dynamics in their relationship began to change. To his surprise, sharing his new response impacted Jean in a very positive way.

Josh was making a statement that communicated that she was worthy enough for him to stand up for her. This was a powerful statement indeed for a woman who had felt invisible and unsupported for most of her life.

Josh and Jean: An Update

They had a blueprint for the work they needed to do to continue their journey. Melva reminded them that having the necessary tools wasn't enough. Each of them had to practice giving what the other had requested. This practice could take three to seven years before they followed through automatically without first thinking it through.

When the positive responses become automatic it is an indication that they have fully developed into positive character traits. Jesse let Jean and Josh know that we were available to coach them until they could do this on their own.

Josh and Jean also knew that the new, healthy behaviors they implemented would help with the other frustrations on their list. Following through would grow, heal and transform them both as individuals as it also deepened and strengthened their relationship.

"When I'm frustrated with Josh," Jean later told us, "I now know what's most and least important to me. That information has really strengthened our marriage. It wasn't like our relationship had broken down, but there were problems in communication. This made a big difference in our comfort level. The beautiful thing is that when we fight he'll ask, 'What can I do to make things better between us?' You've got to love a man who can do that!"

"Aren't I wonderful?" Josh replied.

CHAPTER 10
JESSE AND MELVA'S STORY
MINING FOR GOLD: THE AUTHORS TELL THEIR STORY

"The authors show how they transformed their own frustrations"

Now it's time to hear the story of Melva and Jesse, who lead the ongoing group sessions and workshops referred to throughout this book. They, too, sit in the circle with other participants and usually tell their story last – which began more than 26 years ago.

This is the second marriage for both. Their own relationship growth and development journey is the foundation upon which they have based their teaching, consulting, and counseling. From their own experience Melva and Jesse know that satisfying, long-term relationships require ongoing personal work as well as recommitment. They have learned that identifying the specific work each of them must do in the Mining for Gold process brings a restored connection, heightened pleasure, and a deeper, more loving bond.

Melva and Jesse are an African-American couple who have raised Jesse's two sons from a previous marriage. Both sons are unmarried adults living in two different states.

Melva is a petite woman who loves to change her hairstyles often and dress with a stylish flair for color. Some call her "Pollyanna" because she has a knack for framing situations in a positive context, insisting that the "glass is one half full, even when it looks and feels empty."

But she acknowledges that hers is not always such an easy perspective to maintain, especially when Jesse pushes her buttons. "It's within other people's relationships where I can become the instant possibility thinker and facilitator."

Jesse is a man of average height with speckles of gray throughout his side-burns. He is often described as easygoing, grounded, and caring. People love to hear him speak because the sound of his voice is soothing and calming. It's the kind of voice you would enjoy listening to on your favorite radio station, announcing the cool jazz selections.

When it was time for Jesse and Melva to share their story, Melva volunteered to go first. She sat comfortably in a floral print chair at the home of Josh and

Jean, and took a few moments with eyes closed to consider their story before speaking.

"Jesse and I met 30 years ago as co-workers in the Detroit Public Schools." Both were employed in the School Community Relations Department. Melva had just married her first husband and the marriage was still in the romantic stage." Jesse was just one of many colleagues with whom she developed working relationships.

"Jesse and I were assigned to neighborhood school office locations, and I became part of a group of friendly and mutually supportive colleagues. During my first four years Jesse and I worked together on several joint projects. Since it was his nature to be supportive of all co-workers through-out the city, he naturally supported me as a new hire."

By the end of her third year on the job Melva had moved out of her former home, filed for divorce, and her marriage was over.

"One month after my divorce, Jesse asked me to join him for lunch. It was the first time the two of us had eaten alone without our co-workers. We planned to be at lunch for one hour, but to our surprise, we left the restaurant three hours later. By the end of those three hours, I had told him all my business and my entire life history."

"I couldn't believe that I had done that. However, now that I think about it, I believe I opened up to him so much because he was such a great listener. He told me a lot about himself as well, which made me feel safe."

Jesse, sitting in the chair next to Melva at the session, was still listening attentively.

"Within those three hours we shifted from being mutually respecting colleagues to instant personal friends," Melva said.

Jesse, looking out at the group, added to Melva's story. "One day around lunchtime, I was sitting in my office when I got the idea of inviting Melva to lunch. I had a lot of respect for Melva. She was a hardworking individual who was committed to helping others, smart, knowledgeable, and extremely competent. So I called and invited Melva to share a bite to eat and she said okay. Little did I know how life-changing that lunch would be."

"Neither did I," Melva inserted. "What I didn't know until a few months after that memorable lunch was that Jesse's marriage was in trouble. He was going through a divorce and trying to get custody of his sons."

Jesse, looking at Melva and in a tone of sadness, added, "My marriage was bad, very bad. I had tried to fix it but it hadn't worked, so I was throwing in the towel. It wasn't an easy decision because the lives of four people were involved—my wife, our two sons, and me. No one knew my pain. I wore a mask—smiling, pretending that everything was okay but inwardly feeling tremendous turmoil. I often didn't want to go home—anticipating what I would have to confront when I arrived. But no matter what, whenever I came home, my sons were always glad to see me. They would run up to me, grab me around my legs, and say that they had been waiting for me to come home. Regardless of how I was feeling, my sons always made me feel better.

"But the pain of my marriage was also real—too painful to talk about until that day at lunch with Melva. For the first time in my life I felt safe enough to open up and share my secrets—to talk about the pain I had been hiding. She listened intently—with empathy and compassion. I paid close attention to every change in her facial expression and I could tell that she was making a sincere effort to hear and understand me not only with her ears, but also with her heart. It was very freeing for me. I felt a weight being lifted from my shoulders. It was like, 'whew.' I could trust Melva. She made me feel that she genuinely cared about what I was feeling, and she made no negative judgments about what I was thinking or feeling. After three hours of pouring out our very souls to each other over lunch that day, we became very close friends."

"I can vouch for that," Melva added. "We supported each other through those difficult times."

"After that initial meeting," Jesse continued, "we continued to talk as friend to friend. The more I shared, the better I coped with my emotional distress about the divorce. Sometimes, I would discuss my various options with Melva. She would listen, ask questions; she acknowledged my attempt to consider everyone's well-being as I moved forward."

"I learned so much about his character as I witnessed how he dealt with his pain and struggles," Melva said. "I was most impressed with how he managed his anger and put most of his energy into doing what was best for his boys. Yet he also found time and energy to support me through my own changes. He helped me to set up housekeeping in my new apartment. He helped me to get through my anxiety attacks in the aftermath of divorce. He soothed, comforted, nurtured, and protected me."

And, she added, both of them began to date other people. "Since we were such close friends, we were able to share the highs and lows of those relationships." She sat back and waited for Jesse to add the next part as if she knew what he was about to say.

"Yes, something else was happening for me. Melva was extremely attractive, and over time I knew that I was attracted to her. I was aware that something was going on, but I would not let myself be aware of it or act on it until after I had handled my business around the divorce. Later, after I had gotten divorced, I shared with her how I felt about her. She wasn't ready to take the relationship to that next level, so I made myself content with our friendship. We continued to be best friends." Jesse sighed, and Melva picked up the story with a gleam in her eyes.

"Yeah, when Jesse told me he was ready to take our relationship to a different level, I was surprised, but I now know that I was scared. I wasn't ready for that kind of connection with my safe friend. The thought of it felt like incest. I dealt with it by telling him that being friends really worked for me. He didn't bring it up again."

During the following year, Melva reported, a new romantic relationship she had begun deteriorated and she finally accepted it wouldn't work. She turned inward to try to get herself more focused and grounded.

"I began to think about what I really wanted in a mate. I got really clear about what character traits would lead me to feeling loved and cared about. Oh, did I have a list of what my dream soul mate would be like! One day, as I revised my list, I thought about how the people in our lives are a reflection of our own character—the good, the bad, and the ugly. So as I reviewed my list of the traits that I wanted in my ideal mate, I began to check the ones that I needed to develop in myself. I had checked so many that I decided to go to work on *me* before trying to find Mr. Right."

After about a year of intense personal work, Melva again reviewed her list.

"Something inside me told me that I already knew this person and that it was Jesse. 'Oh, no, this can't be. Jesse is my friend!' This was what I kept telling myself. Then someone else who knew me very well told me they knew that Jesse was the perfect mate for me. She was right. I was too scared to admit it. It took a while for me to tell myself the truth and to finally accept it."

"But what was I to do? Jesse wasn't going to bring the subject up again, since I had turned him down about a year before. So I gathered up my courage and invited him over to dinner."

They sat through dinner, they finished dinner, they even cleaned up the dishes, and still Melva did not tell Jesse what was in her heart. She knew the evening was going to end before she spoke her mind, unless she opened her mouth. Heart pounding, she finally managed to say, "You know that conversation we had a year ago? Well, I've changed my mind. I would like us to change our relationship."

Jesse didn't have the slightest clue that she was ready to be more than friends, and for a few moments he just sat there. Melva said, "It seemed like an eternity, but it couldn't have been more than a few seconds."

"I was surprised—shocked—and happy," Jesse quickly added. "I had no idea what was going on in his mind at the time," Melva said, "and I didn't know that it took him a few moments just to get over the shock and try to collect himself. I just heard a deafening silence that seemed to last forever. All I knew was that he didn't say anything."

Finally, after she couldn't stand it anymore, Melva asked him to say something—anything.

"I was dying inside. Within moments I had made up so many stories in my head. I immediately began to think that he had changed his mind and that I had just made a big fool of myself. Or that he had a new relationship and hadn't told me about it. But I couldn't understand why he hadn't told me, because after all, I was his best friend."

"What seemed like hours later" according to Melva, Jesse finally turned to her and spoke "in a voice I could barely hear."

"I never thought that I'd ever hear you say that. Yes, Melva, I'd like that."

Thus began the romantic stage for Melva and Jesse. They went to dinner, to see movies together, and to nightclubs to dance.

Melva remembered that they talked and talked and talked, as we planned our future with each other and Jesse's sons. "We catered to each other. We laughed a lot and played a lot. We shared many, many wonderfully romantic times together."

And the first time Jesse called her "Honey," Melva said, "I didn't know what to do or say. I think I blushed. I could not get my own tongue untied enough to call him that."

They also began to deepen their professional partnership, teaching relationship classes and providing relationship counseling. "There was a demand for our services, and we rose to the occasion together," Melva said.

At the same time, both of them were individually committed to healing their own pain. Each brought unfinished business into the marriage from previous relationships, including those in childhood. "We were aware that we had some emotional baggage, and we both made a commitment to do the work necessary to make our marriage succeed."

Jesse leaned back in his chair with a smile and straightened his navy blue shirt.

"Most often, love relationships start when two people meet, are attracted to each other, and start dating. Our relationship started quite differently. It began with an innocent invitation of a colleague for lunch, which sparked the ignition of a very meaningful, long-term, close, and mutually supportive friendship. Over time our respect, trust, appreciation, and love for each other grew. They both agreed that even after they decided to take their relationship to the romantic level, their commitment to being each other's very best friends remained steadfast. "We became passionate and loving friends."

"We enjoyed being together. We could be alone in either of our apartments with a bottle of good wine just talking – or not talking – just listening to music. Or we could be happy among our friends at the neighborhood nightclub. It really didn't matter—we liked spending time together. We talked about everything—our childhoods, going to school, old boyfriends and girlfriends, major life decisions we had made, accomplishments, mistakes, hopes and dreams. Nothing was taboo. The more I learned about Melva, the more I learned to respect and appreciate her and the deeper my love for her grew."

Jesse said that his sons soon made their feelings known about their dad's new relationship. On Mother's Day, after church, they asked if they could stop and buy some flowers from a street vendor. "I said 'yes', and asked to whom they were going to give them. Since their birth mother was in another state I thought they might be planning to give them to me.

"Well, that wasn't the case. They told me they wanted to give them to Melva. So we called and asked if we could stop her apartment. I will never forget the scene—my sons standing in front of her door, ringing the doorbell. When she opened the door and the boys presented her with the flowers and said, 'Happy Mother's Day.' I watched Melva lose it. She stood there crying and sobbing all over the place while they hugged. We knew then that it was time for us to start planning to get married."

Melva was slightly teary as she listened to Jesse. "That was the good part," she said with a giggle. "Now's it's time to talk about some of the places where we get stuck. Believe it or not, there were one or two places where we continually got tripped up or bogged down, before we started using this process."

From Romance to Frustration

Jesse continued. "We knew that our getting stuck in reactive behaviors wasn't a question of whether we loved and cared for each other. The issue was figuring out how to manage living together on a day-to-day basis. We had to learn how to deal with each other's little idiosyncrasies instead of letting our frustrations escalate into a major blowup.

"We had to figure how to restore connection after the intense romantic feelings had given way to the day-to-day drudgery of chores and family responsibilities. Family differences can lead to a power struggle over who gets heard and whose needs get met when, and in what order. We thought we were prepared because we had worked so hard beforehand to develop a process to handle all that. However, we were less prepared than anticipated."

They were still trying to figure out ways of managing their frustrations when Melva saw Harville Hendrix on an Oprah Winfrey show. The two attended one of his weekend workshops and, Jesse said, "The experience was life changing. It gave us additional tools to communicate, describe, explain, and resolve our issues when we got stuck."

They then shared with the group a specific example of their process.

Jesse Mining for Gold

Digging beneath the Surface Frustrations for a More Meaningful Connection

Melva looked up from her notes and said to Jesse, "It's your turn to go first. I went first last time."

"No problem. I'm ready."

"Oh-oh!" Melva said. "Since you are a person who usually avoids talking about frustrations, I may be in trouble." Then she took a deep breath. "Okay, I'm ready to hear you."

Describe the Surface of the Conflict

Jesse faced the group and began. "One of my frustrations is around time."

"Time?" Melva interrupted. "You have an issue with time? Oops! It's not my time to speak. Okay, I'm listening." She sat back in her chair, placing her folded fingers under her chin.

Jesse sighed. "As I was saying, I have a frustration around time. Today is a typical example. It was time for us to do something, and Melva was still working on something else, so I had to wait for her, and I didn't like it one bit. I must admit that the tables are now turned. For years I was the one who was always late; then I made a conscious decision to change once I understood my own unhealthy reasons and how being late was disrespectful to others, especially Melva. So, I guess that having to wait on her is a payback for all those years she had to wait on me."

Melva sat quietly but communicated with raised eyebrows, looking perplexed.

Jesse continued. "Another aspect of this time issue is that we have taken on much more than we have time to get done. So, we are often scrambling around trying to get everything done at the last minute. I don't always like working in a pressure cooker and not being able to get things done or be places on time."

Jesse continued looking at the group, not at Melva.

"The time issue between Melva and me is a serious enough problem by itself. An added dimension for me is my inability to discuss the issue without her becoming extremely angry. If I try to address the issue with her, it doesn't get discussed or resolved because I must first deal with her anger and a recapitulation of all the times in our past when she was angry in similar situations. I really don't like being dumped on, criticized, and reminded of every transgression I have ever committed. So I become angry in response to her anger. But rather than letting the situation escalate out of hand, I just shut down. I withdraw emotionally and often physically, by going into another room. I become quiet and incommunicative. Because we have overextended ourselves with projects, I can throw myself into my work. I learned to do this as a child and have continued to do it as an adult." Jesse lapsed into silence for several minutes. His eyes were closed. Knowing the next step, he took his time.

Dig for the Underlying Feelings

What is the Hurt Underneath Your Anger?

He opened his eyes and looked at Melva, who was by then sitting up straight in her chair.

Softly he said, "I feel hurt about two things: One, what is troubling and important to me isn't being heard, and when you don't hear me we can't resolve conflict. That is painful to me. And two, the issue that I put on the table for discussion does not get addressed because it must take a back seat to your anger and all the reasons why you are angry. Your anger then becomes prominent and my feelings get buried beneath what feels like an onslaught of criticism. This is also painful to me because whatever is upsetting me does not get addressed."

Jesse paused. Melva maintained eye contact with him and quietly listened.

What was the Fear Underneath Your Hurt?

"I know describing the fear is next. I just need time to shift gears." Jesse was quiet again for a couple of moments, his eyes closed. When he opened his eyes, he looked at Melva and said, "My fear is that you will take this present situation to add to the list of previous examples of when I disappointed you and that we'll never get to a resolution. You'll get angrier, and I will continue to withdraw. If that happens, we could stay disconnected and unresolved, and that does not feel good. My greatest fear is being emotionally or physically abandoned, or both. When I experience an onslaught of your anger, I feel emotionally abandoned because I am not being heard or understood."

He broke eye contact with Melva and sat back in his chair, looking down.

What are your earliest memories of similar hurts and fears?

"I am very clear about what this reminds me of from growing up," Jesse said. "I remember quite vividly as a child how I tried, most often in vain, to get my mother to hear what I was trying to say. The more I tried, the more agitated she would become. I could not get her to understand or acknowledge my point of view; therefore, I could never win an argument with her. So I was left having to deal with my emotions by myself. I felt abandoned, disconnected, and unsupported, and it felt awful and painful.

"Before we learned how to use the tools that we teach," Jesse added, turning to Melva, "I experienced these same feelings with you when I had something important to discuss and couldn't seem to get you to hear me. The harder I tried, the angrier you got. I didn't feel that I was heard, and I simply couldn't win an argument with you. You have a memory that would rival an elephant's. You don't forget anything and can run down a list of every time I have done something that has upset you. I don't have that kind of memory, so I can rarely explain or defend myself. So I'm left having to deal with my emotions alone, feeling hurt, angry, misunderstood, abandoned, and unresolved, like I did when I was a child.

"Now that you are much better at hearing me out and we address only one issue at a time, I don't have to deal with trying to win an argument."

Find the Gold Nugget: Identify Your Wants and Desires

Jesse said that there was still more work to do, so he went ahead and identified his global desire with regard to this issue of time.

"My global desire is that in spite of how you might be feeling in the moment that you will always take the time to listen to every word I have to say, and that you never, ever, get angry with me again." He smiled, thinking about how great that would feel, and then continued.

"My more realistic desire is that I want us to continue using these tools to discuss what is important to me in a way that makes me feel heard and understood and that leads to resolving the issue to our mutual satisfaction."

Forge the Golden Keys: Ask for What You Want

It was time for Jesse to translate his desires into specific requests.

"I do have three specific ways that I would like you to hear what I have to say. My first request is, for the next 30 days, if I come to you and tell you that there is something important that I want to discuss, that you agree to make an appointment with me to discuss it within 24 hours."

He explained further. "And when I share my concern that you listen without interrupting me until I have finished. Finally, that you not respond to me until 24 hours later, after you have had time to think about what I have shared."

"My second request is, for the next 30 days, when I come to you to share something that I tell you is important to me, that you repeat back exactly what I have said so that I am assured that you have been listening to me."

"My third request is, for the next 30 days, should you become angry with me about something, that for each thing you are angry about you also express two other things that you appreciate about me. And I want you to deliver your appreciations with more emotional intensity than you express your anger."

Jesse had identified his requests to Melva on the way to the meeting, so Melva was prepared to rank them as easy, hard, or extra hard.

"For your first request," she said, I don't have a problem with making an appointment and hearing you out. I have that part down. What I have difficulty with is waiting another 24 hours before I can respond. I want to talk right after I hear you out. So waiting 24 hours I would rank as between very hard and not quite extra hard, meaning that it would be quite a stretch.

"With your second request, if you come to me and let me know that you have something important you want to share, I could repeat it back because you have prepared me to listen. I am almost tempted to pick this one.

"Your third request is between easy and hard. I can identify two things I appreciate for each single thing I am angry about. That part is easy. However, delivering the appreciation with the same intensity as my anger when I have not worked it through—that would be hard and would take a lot of practice. I mean it would take lots of practice, and lots of time!

So, the one I would offer as my gift to you is the first one. For the next 30 days, when you come to me and want to discuss something important, I will grant you an appointment within 24 hours. No problem. I will listen without interrupting and repeat back what I hear you say, tell you how what you are saying makes sense to me, and then tell you how I imagine you are feeling. It is a big stretch for me to wait 24 hours before I respond. But I'll do it."

Jesse nodded. "I like that," he said.

Unlock and Open the Golden Door: Identify the Positive Payoffs for Each Partner

Jesse was ready to accept Melva's gift. "Thank you," he said. "Receiving this gift will help me to continue to heal my feeling of not being heard, and help prepare me for hearing you and responding in a more positive and consistent way. It's amazing how each time we do this, I feel a healing at a deeper level."

It wasn't the first time Melva had taken an opportunity to shift to a new caring and loving response and replace one that had frustrated Jesse.

"You are welcome," she said. "Granting you this gift will help me to stretch my ability to contain my impulse to share my side and to think about your experience longer. It will also increase my ability to self-soothe during the 24-hour period."

Jesse smiled. He reached over and took Melva's hand. They paused for a few moments and then he said to her, "I am ready to hear you now."

The Same Situation, Two Different Experiences: Melva's Reality

Describe the Surface of the Conflict.

Melva had worksheets in her lap. She put them on the table in front of her and began to share her frustration about the same situation. "This is a perfect example of two realities around the same issue. Jesse was triggered because he didn't feel heard and he experienced my anger. I was frustrated and angry because Jesse let me down today."

Turning to Jesse, she said, "It was so interesting to me that you got so upset about me not being ready to leave when you were. I agree with you that through most of our premarital time and more than 20 years of our marriage, I have had to wait for you, and I didn't like it at all. It wasn't just one time I had to wait; it was just about every time we had someplace to be together. We would set a time to leave, and I would be the only one ready. It was refreshing to hear you admit that."

This, time, she acknowledged, *she* wasn't ready. "When you were ready to go, even though I was dressed, I was in the midst of my own frustration. In the moment, I was focused on trying to finish a project by myself that you had promised we would do together. I was frustrated because you didn't help me. You didn't indicate when you might help me, and you had the nerve to be impatient with me! And I was frustrated with myself because I had too much on my plate. The bigger frustration I had was depending on you when you didn't follow through."

"Marriage, to me, is about interdependence, meaning we show up for each other. When you don't show up for me, I feel overwhelmed and angry— angry at me and angry with you. And I know that the way I expressed my anger probably sounded like an onslaught of criticism of you."

Jesse was leaning on his elbow, one finger resting on his temple. "Yes it did," he immediately concurred.

"That's right," Melva responded, "It may have sounded like criticism to you. I know I said something like, 'What do you mean you're ready! How come you get time to take care of you when I'm taking care of all this by myself?'

"My tone probably was terse and biting, I admit that. But that wasn't the first thing. The first thing I do when I get triggered is to get quiet. I don't say anything to you." Melva explained that in the past, her frustration would smolder and simmer inside until it built up to anger and finally a verbal explosion."

"That's because the more I thought about it, the more frustrated I felt and the angrier I got. By the time I got to the verbal explosion, I would let you have it, front to back, side to side. I'd even swear sometimes. Those were the earlier years of our marriage."

Melva acknowledged that while telling Jesse off, she would bring up all the ways he had frustrated her "from day one."

"I really did remember them all because you would not address them. You would just get angry, which didn't make sense to me." Neither strategy worked, she said to the group, "so, I took another route." Melva was talking faster and her eyes lit up as she moved her hands back and forth.

"As the years went by, I would get quieter and not say anything until my anger was more contained. Or, I would verbally snap at him with a tone that clearly communicated that I was irritated. When that didn't work, my reaction might be to get really busy and pretend he was not there. I could even stay up all night, and work through the next day. So if we had issues that I was too angry to talk about, I just went to work. I worked out my anger by distracting myself."

Melva said she responds differently since learning the Mining for Gold process. She sets an appointment and goes through the same kind of dialogue they encourage the other couples to use.

"So today I was quiet until I could get clear about what was really going on with me. I think I am still processing all of it."

Dig for the Underlying Feelings

Since they were on their way to the meeting, though, Melva said, "I had to deal with it. On the drive over I was able to say to Jesse that underneath my anger was the hurt of feeling let down and disappointed. I told Jesse that what hurts more is when he doesn't get it, even though I know he was trying to. It is clear to me that the reason he doesn't get it is because he begins to interpret my experience based on his own reality. But they are so different! He doesn't understand, even though he insists that he does. This is where we have similar wounds. I don't feel understood. I try to explain what is going on with me. Jesse says he understands, but I don't feel that he does. Or, he'll say that he'll follow through in a different manner and then not do it. When this happens, I feel invisible and discounted. I fear having to depend on someone. I don't like feeling needy. Those are the times that I truly don't want to need anything from anyone."

Melva's voice softened and her words came more slowly. She was getting to deeper levels of feeling.

What are Your Memories of Similar Hurts and Fears?

"I have many memories of this hurt and fear," she continued. "Many, many times I have shared with Jesse that there is a connection between my feeling let down, disappointed, misinterpreted, and angry with him and how it relates to the many times my parents disappointed me when I was growing up. It was devastating when they told me they were going to provide me with something I really needed and then, at the last minute, would said they couldn't do it. They would promise to give me money for something I needed. I would be so happy when they would say yes. I would tell my friends I was going to participate, my heart would be set on it, and for some reason they would not follow through. One or two times would have been understandable. But this happened constantly. These incidents began when I was about 12 years old and continued until I quit my first year of college and started working at age 19.

"During my middle and high school years, my mother went in and out of what I now understand may have been bouts of depression. It was such a big shift because she had been so active before—the Brownie leader, the Girl Scout leader, the Y-teen leader. That abruptly stopped. There were times she couldn't even get out of bed. Those were times I needed moral support, but she had a very difficult time giving it."

"During that same period my father got tighter and tighter with money. He encouraged me to participate in activities. That was the good news. I was in a social club, in after-school sports, and in service organizations. He seemed to be proud of me when I became a cheerleader and was voted 'first princess' for homecoming. The bad news was that all of those activities cost money. When I asked him for just the bare bones basics of what I needed, he would say no or he would say yes and at the last minute renege. For high school graduation I had to decide between having a high school ring or sweater. He wouldn't pay for both. My older sister didn't have to make that decision.

"My debutante ball, which was supposed to be a memorable event, became another disappointment. At the last minute, even though he had promised me, he told me that he didn't have money for my dress. This was after months of rehearsal with my friends and our dates. I was humiliated when I had to stay at home on that important night.

"The unfulfilled promises continued into college. My father agreed to support me to attend college. For the first term, he told me at the last minute that he didn't have the money for me to register. That time my mother talked to him, and he came up with the tuition. The last straw was when he told me at the last minute that he didn't have money to pay for my second term. My Uncle Joe came through then and saved the day for me."

"Even though all of those situations hurt, I learned to handle them. I knew I could not change anybody's behavior. That was the foundation for my decision to be independent and not need anyone for anything."

She added – in a softer voice – that after she graduated from college, her father apologized for all the disappointments and asked for her forgiveness. "He finally got it."

Before Jesse and Melva became a couple, she said, "I began to change my mind about being totally independent because Jesse showed up for me by following through in so many ways. During the early part of our marriage, I could still count on him, except when it came to being on time. My core issue with him is about making promises he doesn't keep, so when I depend on him in very specific areas, he often will follow through...but not always."

Melva turned to Jesse and began to state her wants and desires.

Find the Gold Nugget: Identify Your Wants and Desires

"What I needed back then," she said, "was to be heard and understood about what was important to me. It would be helpful to at least have an explanation for the no's, and some idea of a plan B, which would have included realistic alternatives instead of false promises.

"So my global desire for you, Jesse, is for you to always follow through on everything that you say that you're going to do, every single time, under all conditions—through rain, snow, and sleet. That way I know I can consistently depend on you." Melva was giggling. "I love this part."

But she knew the next step. "Okay, I'll do the realistic one. My present desire is for you to follow through when you make promises to me. Otherwise, don't commit. This works better for me than you reacting to me getting upset and disappointed with you."

Jesse nodded.

Forge the Golden Keys: Ask for What You Want

It was time for Melva to put her desires into positive, specific, time-measured, and doable behaviors.

"My first request is for the next 30 days, when I say that I am feeling hurt because you let me down when I depended on your help, I want an appointment to talk about it within 24 hours. And I want you to hear me out until I finish my side of the story. Then I want you to tell me why what I am feeling makes sense to you, and what other feelings you imagine I may have."

"My second request is when I express my anger about you not helping me as you promised, for you to acknowledge aloud that you know there is hurt underneath and that you want to hear about the hurt and talk about a plan to do something about it."

"My third request is that within the next 30 days, when I get angry, I want you to hear me out until I get to the part about how discounted, invisible, disappointed, misunderstood, or just plain scared I feel. And I want you to validate those feelings."

It was time for Jesse to rank Melva's requests and select one to give to her as a gift.

"The first one is hard but doable, because I know about your history before you met me, as well as your history with me. I really do want to follow through. Sometimes I just can't follow through as quickly as I have planned in my mind. So this is hard."

"The second one is hard, but not as difficult as it would have been in the past before I worked toward dealing with your anger. While I understand it, I still have a challenge hearing and dealing with it."

"The third one is extra hard," he continued, "because of the reasons I stated before."

Jesse and Melva were facing each other, eye to eye and knee to knee. Jesse told her that he chose number one.

"For the next 30 days, when you tell me that you are hurt and want to talk, I will grant you an appointment within 24 hours. I will hear you out, tell you what makes sense to me about what you have shared, and tell you what other feelings I imagine you might have."

Unlock and Open the Golden Door: Identify the Positive Payoffs for Each Partner

The next step was for Melva to acknowledge Jesse's gift and to share with him the healing that was likely to take place for her when he followed through.

"Okay, I know there's a healing here somewhere. Hmmmm. Here we go. Granting me this gift will help me to overcome feelings of being devalued, let down, disappointed, and misinterpreted. What I will feel instead is a sense of trust to depend on you to hear me out when you don't follow through.

"I have done a really good job of depending on myself, and that will continue. But the next stage is to add to the ways that I depend on you. You are and have been a very important part of my spiritual and emotional development—not the core, but a very important part of the foundation. You can support me in ways that no one else can or has ever tried to do. And I realize that no one can support me in the ways I need to support myself. It doesn't have to be 'either-or.' I'm talking about 'both-and.' Does that make sense?"

Jesse and Melva held hands and leaned into each other.

"Yes, you do make sense, and I know there is growth for me, too," Jesse said. "My granting you the gift of talking to you, making sense out of your reality, and imagining your feelings will enable me to step outside of myself and understand what you are feeling and experiencing. That will enable me to stretch into looking past myself to really understanding you and doing a better job of trying to meet your needs."

"You know how important that is to me because of your importance to me. I really want to be a good husband and partner for you in every possible way. All I have ever wanted was to enhance your life—to be a blessing to you. Because I love you and want the very best for you."

Melva and Jesse: An Update

"Jesse still triggers me and pushes my frustration buttons from time to time," Melva said when reporting back to the group at a later session. "However, I respond proactively more often than I do reactively. What I mean is, the MFG process works for me to more effectively get my message and point across. I don't ignore the impact of his frustrating behavior, but I share my experience with him before my feelings simmer and smolder to the boiling point."

"I take the time I need to get clear about what is going on with me. Usually what I get in touch with is the fact that I have bought into an illusion created by our unconscious dance. I get excited about a million things and decide, unrealistically, that we can take all of it on at once. I invite Jesse to join me, and in his desire to be on board as a teammate, Jesse signs on. Even against his best judgment, he agrees to participate. I blast away full steam ahead until I get to a place where I either run out of energy or don't know what to do, or both. Then I look for Jesse's help. Jesse, overwhelmed from what he is already taking care of, says 'yes.' However, he can't get to it right away because he's working on several other projects. Then we hit deadlines that we miss and I get anxious and put pressure on Jesse. He hears it as criticism or demands, and it makes him feel unappreciated."

"I feel disappointed and let down, and we go around and around on the surface. So when Jesse describes what he experiences as intense anger and criticism from me when he is already trying to do his best, I honor that, because he makes sense to me."

Jesse added, "I know I don't always initiate or follow up as much as I would like to, and that is something I'm working on. Melva is much better at multi-tasking than I am, and I know she might forget sometimes that I don't function at her rapid pace. I appreciate that she understands that I have a slower and more deliberate rhythm when getting things done. And that I am sincere when I commit, but when I over-commit, I can't keep up. But we know that it isn't a matter of good or bad, just different. We each have our own pace, and we each need to do things in our own time."

Melva said, "I am pleased with how we continue to deal successfully with whatever comes up between us. And we have a mindset of curiosity about the vulnerable and undeveloped places within us we are trying to grow and develop to a higher level. It empowers us and it improves the health of our relationship."

"I can also see how we both co-create the past within the present, and how we sabotage aspects of our commitment and covenant to being together as a couple."

"Being really clear about what lies beneath the surface for both of us takes us to a goldmine of opportunity to experience love and care at the deepest level. That is what I have learned and why I am very excited about this. There is probably a part of me that is a little apprehensive, as well. So my mantra is that I am increasing my capacity to give and receive more love. Utilizing the MFG process for dialogue enriches me, because each time we share our realities from a place of compassionate understanding it not only produces healing and growth, but it also makes me feel a little bit transformed."

Jesse continued, "Yes, we truly have experienced the benefits of Mining for Gold in our ever-evolving marriage. We know that it restores our connection in a way that deepens intimacy. As we continually process the 'golden nugget' into 'golden keys' that consistently keep the 'golden door' open to giving and receiving the love that nurtures both of us, our relationship evolves to healthier levels of true intimacy."

CHAPTER 11
UNCOVERING THE GOLD WITHIN YOUR RELATIONSHIP

You Too Can Strike Relationship Gold

Throughout this book our primary objective was to capture the intrinsic value – the hidden gold – available to us within the journey of a committed love relationship…specifically, marriage.

As we said earlier, committed love relationships are designed to go through three predictable stages: 1) romance, 2) frustration and conflict, and finally, 3) mature love. The challenging second stage provides the opportunity for couples to discover a deeper connection, a more meaningful, enjoyable, satisfying, and happier relationship of significant worth and value—the "gold." To succeed, couples must have a way of managing their reactivity to dig beneath their surface issues to meet the unfulfilled needs each have brought into their relationship. The MFG process is one such tool.

Mining for Gold is a metaphor for one of the most powerful processes that we know of for tapping into the phenomenal potential of that stage, which can be the hardest and the most valuable experience for each partner.

We believe that the power comes from the step-by-step conversational process. This dialog of intimacy creates a safe environment for couples to interrupt common, frustrating styles of reactive behavior directed toward one another. Such reaction fuels conflict and keeps couples stuck and miserable on the surface.

The time, energy and commitment it takes to dig beneath the surface of those frustrations is worth the effort, because it leads to the priceless gold nuggets. To mine effectively, you have to apply the process consistently enough to have an initial breakthrough and identify the hidden, undeveloped, or underdeveloped potential of each partner.

Digging beneath the superficial surface of a relationship in this way becomes a system for mutual nurturing, affirmation, respect, support, healing, and growth for the couple. Once identified, those mined nuggets can repair any damage caused by feelings of ruptured connectivity.

The continuation of the process provides meaning, which captures our vision of possibility and potential. Insight, energized by actual feelings of connection, opens the door and allows us to enter into and embrace interaction as a foundation for stage three, the maturation of love. This is the stage where the relationship a couple shares can blossom and thrive.

Such potential is easily accessible during the attraction and romantic stages of the relationship. But we want couples to understand that the real work begins after the honeymoon. It is then when couple's are presented with ongoing opportunities through their conflicts to mine the promise and the greater possibilities their relationship holds for them.

Even using the tools we teach, partners will sometimes unintentionally frustrate each other and will not see eye to eye. However, based upon our own personal experience and those couples whom we've guided through the process we have seen the MFG process transform relationships. This tool can help couples to successfully understand the bigger picture and interpret important messages that exist beneath ongoing reactive patterns of behavior.

Once we are adequately equipped with information and awareness, we can decide to follow through and articulate those uncovered messages in a way that supports living together in a mutually satisfying relationship. The upset feelings do not have to simmer to a boiling point until one or both partners throw in the towel and call it quits.

We emphasize creating a safe, calm environment to engage in MFG because when one or both partners are emotionally triggered, success is more difficult and challenging. A calm, safe, interactive environment is required to dig beyond the surface to unfold and decode the bigger picture of the vulnerability and pain buried in the unconsciousness. Decoding the bigger picture reveals a blueprint for excavating the gold found in stage three.

Sharing and listening in this structured manner is the process through which each partner can overcome their internal barriers and change words and behaviors that frustrate into ones that nurture.

The process is sustained by a commitment to take the time necessary to look at the "cause and effect" within, while exploring the impact of the frustrating behavior of one's partner. It is difficult at times to own up to, and take responsibility for, our part in perpetuating the conflict and then getting stuck and staying entrenched. It isn't easy to be honest with ourselves about how we frustrate, irritate, hurt, and/or scare our partners.

Understanding and taking responsibility are major stepping stones toward establishing internal safety, which is a fundamental prerequisite for delving into the dynamics of the conflict, the deeper meaning, and the lessons to be learned about ourselves and our partners. The intent isn't to open the door to wallow in self-criticism or blame. On the contrary, the goal is healing and intimacy.

And it is twofold. First we unearth and embrace the vulnerable parts of ourselves. We try to address them and heal from the pain that comes from hurtful interactions that wound us during the expression of our frustrations.

Secondly, our intent is to honor and stretch into the growth of an important part of ourselves, in order to reach a relationship skill level that nurtures, supports and empowers us within the context of marriage.

These two rewards come from "staying the course, digging deep and working it out." We then begin to co-create precious memories that generate good feelings about our past, present, and future experience.

Changing behavior in a way that meets the needs, longings, and heartfelt desires of each partner to feel loved and cared about improves the focus and quality of a relationship. The process also guides each partner to function at a higher level as an adult in a committed love relationship. The stretching, healing and growth that occurs increases each individual's capacity to give and receive love at a deeper level.

In this respect, MFG is also a metaphor for an effective process for growing to mature love. Each step on the journey is a step toward becoming the best partner you can be in your relationship. Being at your best puts you in the ideal situation to invite your partner to be at their best. Functioning at your optimum fosters a deeper feeling of closeness for both.

Witnessing couples strike gold mines of untapped potential in their relationships has been fascinating for us. And we recall the warmth we felt within when we chose to follow this process ourselves and enjoy the positive payoff.

"Practice makes perfect," and that is certainly true for the Mining for Gold process. Utilizing the tools of the MFG process is compared to striking gold because enjoying a loving and caring relationship is priceless.

When we understand how behaviors such as avoiding, criticizing, demanding, blaming, yelling, screaming, leaving, throwing things, threatening, playing victim, overeating, overworking, or attempting to numb the pain through drugs or alcohol hurt and wound our partner – in other words, the behaviors that don't solve anything – we gain leverage from a place of empathy. We are able to change, rather than continue to compound a bad situation and make it worse through reactivity.

Once we know about the opportunity to mine for the gold, we no longer have to ask ourselves if we chose the right partner. We no longer question why we didn't see all of those frustrating behaviors in the beginning. We had those behaviors too. But during the romantic stage, we also had the help of nature's endorphins to keep them at bay.

Rather than focusing solely on changing our partner, we have sufficient understanding of what to concentrate on within ourselves that needs to change. We understand our contribution to – and collaboration with – the problem.

We also understand that whether we stay or leave, we will take our style and pattern of hurtful defensive reactive behaviors with us to the next relationship. If there is abuse or other danger, we owe it to ourselves to get out of that kind of relationship and into a safe space. However, if those are not factors in our marriage and we leave the relationship prematurely, we miss the opportunity to develop more mature relationship skills. Then our growth and development as persons and partners continues to be arrested. We see the process as a chance to dig deeper, so that we don't continue to co-create a situation that won't go away but simply recurs in other relationships because it has not been worked out and resolved.

Mature love entails having an effective process for working through frustrations and conflicts, so that couples spend more time engaged in the rich loving and caring behaviors that nurture and support a strong foundation for a lasting and priceless relationship.

Although this process is relatively easy to understand, it takes energy, courage, and motivation to successfully implement it and reap the benefits. However, as we have described, the payoff for all the difficult prospecting, digging, and exploration is a personal stake in an unlimited mine of relationship gold.

For our illustrations we purposefully selected couples that were not in serious trouble, because we wanted to point out that daily frustrations, if left unattended, can wreak relationship havoc. However, in many cases, this process also works for couples in serious trouble.

The MFG is one of the most effective relationship processes we have taught. During our 30 years of working together, we have seen it succeed with hundreds of couples and individuals. We are grateful for the powerful, life transforming impact we have observed.

Some of the couples we worked with were at the brink of ending their union, but were able to restore it. Some painful relationships, like Nina and Michael's, didn't work out. But they did end respectfully. And some individuals, after using the process alone, gained a way of communicating that respected and honored their partners as well as themselves.

One participant decided to attend one of our workshops on the basis of changes he had witnessed in the life of one of his relatives. He said, "I know how bad things were with them. Now when I see them and how happy they are, I want to cry. And I want what they've got."

Our MFG metaphor is what Harville Hendricks calls, "Turning Frustrations into Behavior Change Requests." It is one of many powerful and transformative tools facilitated for hundreds of thousands of couples by over 2000 certified Imago Relationship Therapists and 200 Certified Imago Couples Workshop Presenters worldwide.

We are honored to be a part of this community of professionals committed to uplifting, healing, growing and transforming couples who, in turn, transform families, communities, and the greater society.

Review of the Mining for Gold Process
Key Points and Lessons from the Seven Stories

There are two possible outcomes for couples in conflict. Each partner can continue to "prove" the other wrong and maintain the conflict. This breaks the connection, which is the foundation of the relationship. Or, they can decide to change the focus of the destructive fighting at the surface in order to dig deep below it and create an environment to restore a loving and caring connection.

Surface of the Conflict – Ben and Ada

Ben and Ada's story taught us that the innocence of timing for sharing exciting good news can trigger an adverse reaction in one's partner. In Ben's case, Ada's timing conflicted with his need for time to relax and escape from the stresses of a hard day's work. That is why staying focused on the topic of the conflict and our partner's possible perception of ill will needs to be explored in more depth. The immediate topic of the conflict rarely leads to the unearthing of the real problem, which is a difference in the needs of each partner at a particular moment. That is what needs to be decoded.

When one partner, like Ben, manages their frustrations by withdrawing, the coping behavior often triggers the other partner, leading to reactions of expressed hurt such as anger, criticism, or leaving the room, as Ada did. A rupture in the feeling of connection occurs.

Like Ben and Ada, couples often experience frustration and think, "Oh my god, I'm feeling THIS again." This feeling is generated by a well tooted arsenal of defensive cause and effect behaviors. The frustrating behavior is the "cause" which triggers the frustrating feeling or the "effect". This leads to a vicious cycle of defensive reactions that stay on the surface.

There is more blaming and shaming of our partner for their behavior, and less taking of responsibility for how our words or behaviors inflict some- times irreparable damage on the psyche of our partner – and therefore their experience and perception of us.

The unsettling cycle leads to the negative consequence of continual negative and reactive defensive behaviors, because each partner feels wounded by the other.

Although the wounding Ada and Ben inflicted on one another damaged their feeling of connection in the moment; the damage wasn't irreparable. The couple was motivated to stop hurting and re-wounding each other, and to move toward their healing and reconciliation journey, mining for the gold beneath the surface.

Preparing the Soil

Identify the Behavior in Your Partner that Triggers an Intense Emotional Reaction in You

Cause and Effect:

We provide a script for couples to communicate their experience safely and to invite the other to listen and hear with compassion. 10% of the descrip- tion is about the partner's frustrating behavior, while 90% of the message describes the internal experience of the Sender.

We start by separating the frustrating behavior of our partner from our frustrating feeling in reaction to it. The specific language of the Sender begins with, "When you _____."

The goal is to describe in one short phrase what your partner said or did that frustrated you.

Identify Your Surface-Level Emotional Feelings and Reactive Behaviors

Follow that phrase with, "I felt _____."

Describe your feeling response. This might include sadness, fear, anger, or rage. This feeling has meaning and leads to an interpretation reflected in our self-talk at both conscious and unconscious levels. There is a story that we tell ourselves about what our partner's words or behaviors mean to us. The meaning is a clue to why and how we react to our partner. The bottom line is whether the Sender perceives the frustrating behavior as safe or dangerous.

At the unconscious and conscious levels, the frustrating behaviors are perceived as a threat. It is the threat that we react to. So when we describe our reaction we are describing how we cope when we feel threatened, which in many cases also involves taking ownership of our role in the conflict.

The third phrase of the sentence is "What I did in reaction to your frustrating behavior was to _____."

Describe what you said or did out of anger, hurt or fear. Did you shut down or lash out? Here is a review of Ada's "Send" at the surface:

"Ben, when I came home excited about telling you about my promotion, you ignored me and just kept looking at television. And when you did this, I felt angry."

What she was telling herself was, "I work hard at the office, and getting some kind of acknowledgement means so much to me. You not listening and celebrating with me means you don't care. So I react by yelling at you."

Ada owned her reactive behavior of yelling at Ben.

A review of Ben's "Send":

"When you yell at me and criticize me, I feel angry. What I tell myself is that you are being selfish and don't care about me. So I react by withdrawing from you."

Ben owned his behavior of withdrawing when he felt overwhelmed and unheard.

Dig for Underlying Feelings Beneath the Reactive Behavior:

Find the Hurt beneath Your Reactive Response

We dig to identify the hurt and fear because beneath the reactive behaviors is our pain. Communicating pain expresses vulnerability. The hurt and fear in the present conflict pulls the scab off of the history of the un-repaired, unhealed hurt and fear- pain that each partner brought into the relationship from somewhere in the past.

Too many couples in conflict rarely get to this step because when one allows one's self to become vulnerable, emotional safety must be assured. Instead of creating an emotional refuge, so much time is spent on the unproductive exchange of what each person said or didn't say, or on what they did or they didn't do.

The Importance of the Pain of Hurt in the Present Conflict
Sophie and Buddy

We believe that when we don't get the love and caring we need from our partner, we experience a sensation of psychological hurt and fear.

Feeling used when she has so many responsibilities is the source of the pain beneath Sophie's behavior of barking out orders to Buddy.

Feeling alone and inadequate as a man, husband, father, and a provider is the hurt that symbolizes the pain beneath Buddy behavior of slamming objects around and withdrawing from Sophie. While he seethes in anger and isolation he needs reassurance that he is okay and that Sophie still believes in him.

The Pain in the Fear
Simone and Michael

Usually during any ongoing conflict there is an underlying fear of some type of catastrophe.

Simone's fear was of not being able to count on Michael when she needed him, which triggers her depression and her drop in self-esteem. Not being able to depend on Michael triggers an additional fear that he doesn't love her enough to give her the emotional nourishment she needs from him. Further, she is afraid that she won't be strong enough to recover from being let down.

The pain in Michael's fear is of being perceived as inadequate and controlled, and of getting very little positive feedback from her about what he is doing right.

The Importance of Making the Connection of Pain in the Present to Childhood Pain in Our Relationship History
Chris and Deborah Ann

Pain of hurt and fear in a current conflict often has its own history. That history entails times in the past when we needed a specific form of love and caring and didn't get it. And the times we did get it are often ignored.

The pain she felt that Chris was not emotionally available organically triggered memories within Deborah Ann of her history with her parents being similarly unavailable. Those memories included living parents who were so self- absorbed in their anger that they didn't notice that she was present and was feeling invisible.

It was important for Chris to know when Deborah relived this feeling, because she had learned to protect herself from feeling the pain by making herself disappear from the situation. Reliving her pain is excruciating because each time she does so, she feels lonely and abandoned.

She chose to, and enjoys, taking care of the children she has with Chris. But she didn't have that choice as a child when she was stuck at home taking care of two little brothers, a responsibility that never afforded the opportunity for her to be a kid herself. Feeling scared while waiting for her parents to come home is relived when she feels scared waiting for Chris. And the same way her parents used to do, Chris sometimes gets home and can't talk to her about the fear in Deborah's heart because he's distracted by his own issues.

Although Deborah Ann's experience of Chris listening to her fears and needs was an important element and a major source of attraction for her, the couple could not sustain it beyond the romantic stage without an intervention to identify and decode the underlying pain.

Chris' pain had roots as well. He grew up with parents who were abusive, negligent, cold and distant. He had a father who was demanding, violent and volatile. He felt an overwhelming and desperate need to please his father in an attempt to gain approval and love. And Chris experienced the pain of neglect from his mother, whom he dearly loved. The feeling of neglect stemmed from her assigning him the role of being her confidante, because his dad didn't listen to her. So the parent-child roles were reversed. The emotional availability he needed for his own growth and development was arrested because he was giving to his mom what he should have been receiving from her.

Although he described the upside of this as an experience that made him a good listener, the downside was a lack of tenderness when he was feeling vulnerable and needed to be listened to. Attention and hugs only occurred when it was time to fulfill his role, and then they felt like a setup for him to perform, which produced within him much confusion and anxiety.

Identifying Your "Golden Nugget"— Knowing What You Want
Mike and Robin

Underneath our day-to-day frustrations and conflicts is a real desire and longing to restore connection. We call this part of the MFG process, "gold nuggets" because in our minds, putting time and energy into identifying and expressing our deepest desires for connection in a loving and caring way gives us a focus for staying on the journey toward stage three.

Starting with a global desire is important because it helps us shift from feeling flooded with the pain of our experience in conflict to a focus upon the potential and possibility embedded in the next steps.

Robin's global desire for Mike to feel that her needs were important to him all the time is fascinating and recaptures that part of us that dreams big. She has gigantic dreams of Mike going dancing with her every week and dancing every dance with her. Isn't it interesting that Mike's global desire is for Robin to say to him that he would never, ever have to dance again and she would still be happy?

Mike bonding with Robin through dance is important because it can help her feel connected to him and declare to the world that "this is my man and we are together." And because it represents a big emotional step for Mike, it also represents a much bigger gift that Robin initially realized.

When you do this step, be sure to share the bigger picture of your desire first. Even though your partner may not necessarily meet that need, you will help them to understand what you long for and you will be more likely to gain the compassion you deserve.

When you are also specific and realistic about what you want, you prepare a blueprint for your partner to replace frustrating behaviors with behaviors that feel loving and caring.

Golden Keys of Asking for What You Really Want
Theodore and Nina

Insight and awareness are important steps because they establish sufficient empathy and compassion to maintain a safe environment for being able to describe and invite behavior that fosters intimacy. Motivation to stop hurtful behaviors can then be provided, along with changes to those specific behaviors that are effective in restoring lost connection. When couples articulate exactly what they want using the Mining for Gold language, they are holding a golden key.

It is important to ask for what we want. And it is crucial to ask in a way our partner can hear. Some may find it difficult to clearly pinpoint exactly what they want in specific behavioral terms and in a way that enhances their chances of receiving a positive response. Such communication is a skill that usually takes time to master. That is why we use the acronym S.M.A.R.T. which stands for short, measurable, achievable, relevant to the situation, and time measured.

And there is a reason why there are three requests rather than only one or two. Three expands the options for choice. There is power in having choices. When our partner has the opportunity to chose, they don't feel controlled or pressured. It is an opportunity for them to perceive that they are granting a gift.

Following through on fulfilling our partner's desire requires stretching and growing into the potential of a hidden or underdeveloped relationship skill within us. That is why it is so important to be clear and communicate how much stretching and growth will take place for us in following through on our relationship gifts.

Arriving at the airport on time and meeting her at the baggage claim when Nia's plane arrived was a hard stretch for Theodore. However, the stretching was more about his embracing a core relationship skill of differentiation – honoring two conflicting realities and needs – his and hers. He was making space to hear what was going on with her while he simultaneously honored what was going on with himself. We cannot emphasize enough how important this step is for turning things around.

Concurrently, every time Nia got angry and did the hard work of stretching into putting her emotions into clear, intelligible words, she held a golden key to doing her part to reverse the situation. It would have been so much easier for her to shut down and hold Theodore's frustrating behavior over his head for a long period of time.

When you do this step, make sure you honor the difficulty of fulfilling the behavior you choose. Both you and your partner need to be fully aware of the level of difficulty you experience in following through on a gift of changed behavior, because this helps to unfold the process into another element of compassion.

Unlocking the Golden Door to Mature Love – Stage III
Unfolding the Potential for Becoming a Source of Safety and
Pleasure to Improve the Quality of the Relationship
Josh and Jean

Following through on our commitments opens the golden door to our own growth and our partner's healing. The growth for us is that we build or strengthen a crucial skill that gives us a blueprint for how to be in a relationship with our partner more effectively.

The healing and repair for our partner is the experience of feeling more loved, validated, and cared for. And just beyond this golden door is where couples experience their deepest, greatest, and most enduring benefits.

Josh and Jean illustrated this principle for us. Every time Jean cut down on how much money she spent on gifts for her daughter and she and Josh agreed on an acceptable amount, she developed the ability to set boundaries with her daughter, something she admits was hard for her to do. But it gave her an essential relationship skill.

The more Jean granted this gift, the more she grew and strengthened her ability to be available to her daughter, to Josh, and to herself. She also gained confidence in her ability to take better care of herself and the people she loves.

Her growth had a healing impact on Josh. He felt more wanted by, and connected to, Jean. This began to repair and heal his current and past pains of not feeling important, approved of, or wanted by people he loved.

Every time Josh validated and emphasized Jean's need to be emotionally available to her daughter he grew, because he had compassion for their special mother-daughter relationship, which, as a result, no longer threatened him. He became more tolerant of Jean's support system of coping with the stressors in her daughter's life. He also began to experience Jean's availability to her daughter as valuable and important, and became a source of emotional availability himself.

His growth had a healing impact on Jean because his support communicated to her that she was valuable enough that someone she loved would stand up for her. When he stood up for her, Jean's history of familiar feelings of being invisible and unsupported begin to dissolve.

When you do this step, be sure to be clear about what relationship skill you will develop when you give your partner their heart's desire. Remember, your growth has a healing impact. This process is not complete until you know what that impact actually is.

Now that you have the golden key to open that golden door to stage three to mine those gold nuggets of your partner's desires and begin to enjoy the relationship of your dreams.

MFG and Conflict Resolution

There will be temptation to revert to old and familiar defensive behaviors. It will feel easier and more convenient to criticize, blame, ignore, yell, and withdraw from your mate when they frustrate you.

However, once a couple has had a successful experience and practices the Mining for Gold process, either alone or with coaching, they have a choice to either fight or mine for the understanding, empathy, and compassion that restores a loving connection. We know from personal and professional experience that implementing these new behaviors consistently can be difficult because we are entering the unexplored territory of arrested growth. But as we heal the pain in our current relationships, we heal what we experienced in our past relationship histories.

New growth does not happen in a flash, and neither does change that leads us away from old growth patterns. A decision to change can be made in an instant, but the growth and learning curve required to successfully achieve a permanent change takes knowledge, skill, time, commitment, persistence and support.

This Mining for Gold process is no instant fix, and going for the golden nuggets is not a get-rich-quick relationship scheme. We encourage couples to be persistent and patient. Permanent change is a slow process and requires patience and tenderness with both yourself and your significant other. But the alternative is to remain stuck in conflict, continue to re-wound each other, neglect emotional scars, and smolder or simmer until the pain becomes so unbearable that there is an emotional and/or physical exit from the relationship.

We have only emphasized one of many powerful processes —the Mining for Gold process—for turning frustrations into behavior change requests. Mining the nuggets leads to the priceless currency no money can buy, namely, growth that supports the unfolding evolution of the expression of our authentic selves.

Imagine you and your partner providing the caring words, behaviors, and touch desired by one other so that both of you feel loved in very specific ways.

Imagine giving and receiving this powerful human expression of affirmation, nurturance, and support that heals, grows, and transcends the ordinary to reach the extraordinary.

Imagine you and your partner as leaders and role models of how to relate for your children, your family, your community, and society at large.

Feeling loved and cared about, we believe, impacts how we function as human beings in all of our various relationships. And it has a ripple effect on those we interact with in both our inner and outer social circles.

While we encourage you to try out this process on your own, we cannot overemphasize the value of seeking help from a trained and competent relationship therapist, if you find yourself stuck.

We highly recommend a certified Imago Relationship Therapist, because they have been trained in all the Imago interventions for restoring connection in relationships.

We encourage this because we know that when couples are able to solve problems successfully on their own, they do. But there should be no stigma around the issue of taking help from trained professional when you don't get the results you desire by yourself. For most of us there are times when assistance is needed to unearth the deeper roots of an impasse. Some couples will say that they cannot afford the help financially.

We say that the financial investment in acquiring tools to help your relationship survive and thrive is priceless. Statistics show that investments in healing and growing your relationship with yourself and your partner are far less costly, both emotionally and financially, than separation or divorce.

Imagine for a moment what is possible for you and your partner if you dig deep enough to reach the golden door to deeper levels of intimacy.

Imagine how new language between the two of you will heal and repair the wounds inflicted during conflicts you've had. Imagine how that language will give voice to deeper communication, where harsh words or stifling silences once existed in your marriage.

Imagine relationship skill development and the possibility for expanded levels of feeling more loved and cared about.

Imagine the role model you can provide for others, especially children and teens who are constantly bombarded by the media with negative and unrealistic images of relationship dynamics.

The gift of experiencing the gold of new loving words and behaviors will most likely be a pleasure to give and to receive. But giving and receiving have their own challenges and issues, for two reasons. The first is that our memories of previous hurts and fears may surface if our partner does not follow through on a commitment. If this happens, you may re-experience your history of pain.

Second, your partner may give you what you want, but you will find something wrong with it. If this happens, it is an opportunity for each person to shift gears to get back on track, taking corrective action. That entails revisiting the MFG process, steps one through four.

It is possible that if you have never had the experience of getting what you want, you may not know what to do with it once it lands in your lap. It is important to make a commitment to yourself to open your heart to the potential and possibility before you, and embrace it as a gift you deserve.

As a couple in a long-term marriage, we have used the process to stay on track, mindful of the areas where we both get stuck. When we hit a snag, we go back into the process because by doing so, it empowers us to successfully move through our most difficult frustrations to create a deeper bond of mutual love, respect, and connection.

We do not mean to imply that we no longer have frustrations with each other. But by faithfully using the process, we are able to sustain a more loving connection for longer and longer periods of time. The "not okay" periods are becoming less frequent and not as intense when they do arise.

Striving to become more of an authentic person who does not inflict pain when frustrated or faced with conflict is important and valuable work. The result is that you become a source of safety and pleasure for yourself and your partner.

The couples in our stories have demonstrated that Mining for Gold is the positive alternative and a better choice. They were able to experience healing and growth that fostered an experience of love and intimacy each had longed for throughout their lives.

Our sincere hope is that the sharing of these journeys has inspired you and given you hope and insight into a new way of deepening the love connection with the significant persons in your life.

ABOUT THE AUTHORS

Jesse and Melva Johnson have more than 60+ years of combined experience helping individuals, couples, families, and groups improve the quality of their relationships.

They have devoted their professional lives to empowering people to identify and embrace the "gold" beneath discord and to transform unproductive behaviors into those that heal, grow, nourish, and encourage healthy relationships. Through decades of training and experience in psychotherapy, counseling, coaching, and consulting, they have assisted hundreds of people to incorporate untapped resources within themselves and their relationships, to co-create positive relationship skills and behaviors.

Melva is a certified Imago Relationship Therapist, Workshop Presenter and former President of the Association of Imago Relationship Therapists. Jesse is certified in a variety of relationship modalities including Imago, and has also served as President-Elect of the Association for two years. From 2001–2005, they co-hosted *Personal Transformations*, a cable TV show that reached a viewing audience of 120,000. The two therapists have been featured in Detroit's largest newspapers and their expertise is often cited in other local print, radio, and television media. Between 2003 and 2006, more than half a dozen features about the Johnsons appeared in the *Detroit News* and the *Detroit Free Press*, which enjoy a combined circulation of over 600,000.

The co-authors have demonstrated the effectiveness of the process they teach in *Mining for Gold* within their own personal and professional relationships. They have worked together as a team before and throughout their marriage. They use MFG regularly within their own relationship to resolve conflicts, prevent the build-up of frustrations, and sustain free-flowing intimacy, passion, and pleasure.

Yes, I Want To Take The Next Step In The Mining For Gold Process

Please have your representative contact me my phone. I would like to know more about how the Mining for Gold process can help me implement the ideas discussed in this book.

My Key Relationship Frustrations are:

- ☐ Communication Problems
- ☐ Lack of Sex - Romance
- ☐ Lack of Commitment
- ☐ Affairs - Cheating
- ☐ Overcoming Resentments
- ☐ Not Enough Time/Attention
- ☐ Dealing With Anger
- ☐ Incompatibility
- ☐ Lack of Emotional Support
- ☐ Blaming/Criticism/Resentments
- ☐ Ex Wife/Husband
- ☐ Blended Family Issues

- ☐ Financial Problems
- ☐ Lack of Trust
- ☐ Parenting Issues
- ☐ Fighting - Arguing
- ☐ Overcoming Hurt
- ☐ Forgiveness
- ☐ Dealing With Jealousy
- ☐ How To Get Unstuck
- ☐ Managing Chores & Duties
- ☐ Making It Last Long Term
- ☐ Other _____
  _____

My Information:

Name:_____

Address:_____

City:_____ State:_____ Zip Code:_____

Email Address:_____

Daytime Phone Number:_____

Fax Number:_____

Your Current Relationship Status is:_____

Three Easy Ways To Contact Us Are:

- Visit Our Website at www.MiningForGoldRelationships.Com
- Fax this completed form to us at (248) 498-6006
- Call us at (877) 552-1161

Personal Transformations
512 S. Washington, Suite 329
Royal Oak, MI 48067

Let Us Help You To
Go For The Gold In Your Relationship